The Needlecraft Shop
Presents

Cross-Stitch

Country Charm

the Needlecraft® Shop

The miracle of cross-stitch stems not from the
artful blending of fabric and thread, but from the pricelessly
precious piece of the stitcher's heart
woven within each strand.

Interim Editorial Director: JANET TIPTON PERRIN
Product Development Manager: FRAN ROHUS
Production/Photo Director:
ANGE VAN ARMAN

EDITORIAL
Senior Editor: NANCY HARRIS
Editor: MARYLEE KLINKHAMMER
Assistant Editor: REBECCA BIRCH MOEHNKE
Product Presentation Copy: JENNIFER MCCLAIN
Copy Editor/Proofreader: SALWAY SABRI

PRODUCTION
Book Design: GREG and MINETTE SMITH
Production Manager: DEBBY KEEL
Color Specialist: BETTY HOLMES
Production Coordinator: GLENDA CHAMBERLAIN

PHOTOGRAPHY
Photography Manager: SCOTT CAMPBELL
Photographers: KEITH GODFREY, ANDY J. BURNFIELD

PRODUCT DESIGN
Publications Coordinator: JANET L. BIRCH
Design Coordinator: TONYA FLYNN

BUSINESS
CEO: JOHN ROBINSON
Vice President/Marketing: GREG DEILY

Dear Friends

Let me invite you to bring the charm of country living into your life with appealing cross-stitch designs. In this book, we've put together a collection of projects from top cross-stitch designers allowing you to add the special feeling of warmth to your home that only a hand-crafted accessory can bring. The basic combination of embroidery floss and fabric become the tools for creating artistic color and design. You become the artist who can easily create the eye-catching projects that fill the pages of this book.

With six charming categories that draw on country themes, you'll enjoy projects for every room and any occasion. *Country Charm* transforms a variety of designs, from humorous to poignant, into lovingly-made pieces you'll be proud to stitch and proud to give as gifts. Why not start right away, and see how charming life can be!

Nancy
Nancy Harris

CREDITS
Sincerest thanks to all the designers, manufacturers and other professionals whose dedication has made this book possible.

Special thanks to
Quebecor Printing Book Group, Kingsport, TN.
Copyright © 1999 The Needlecraft Shop, LLC

Library of Congress Cataloging-in-Publication Data
ISBN: 1-57367-109-6
First Printing: 1999
Library of Congress Catalog Card Number: 99-75971
Published and Distributed by
The Needlecraft Shop, LLC, Big Sandy, Texas 75755
Printed in the United States of America.

Contents

Country Charm

Country Gardens

Chapter One

Country Humor

Chapter Two

Country Fantasy

Chapter Three

General Instructions

Country Christmas
Chapter Four

Country Inspirations
Chapter Six

Country Autumn
Chapter Five

Stand among the blossoms of a
garden at dawn and listen gently to
the symphony of Nature resounding
from the dew-kissed petals.

Country Gardens

Tenderly the needle guides the thread,
bringing life to the stitches like the feathery strokes
of a paintbrush caressing the canvas of an artful masterpiece.

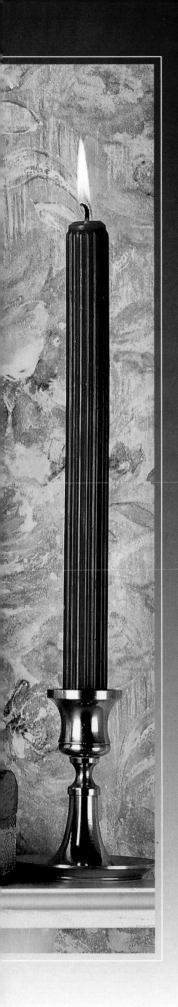

Everything Is Beautiful

Designed by Gail Bussi

Materials
- 13" x 14" piece of antique white 28-count Jobelan®

Instructions
Center and stitch design, stitching over two threads and using two strands floss for Cross-Stitch and one strand floss for Backstitch and French Knot.

Stitch Count:
98 wide x 108 high

Approximate Design Size:
11-count 9" x 9⅞"
14-count 7" x 7¾"
16-count 6⅛" x 6¾"
18-count 5½" x 6"
22-count 4½" x 5"
28-count over two
  threads 7" x 7¾"

Soothe your soul and calm your mind with the enchantingly thought-provoking beauty of this timeless design, quietly proclaiming its ageless wisdom.

X	B'st	½x	DMC	ANCHOR	COLORS		X	B'st	½x	Fr	DMC	ANCHOR	COLORS		X	B'st	½x	DMC	ANCHOR	COLORS
			#223	#895	Victorian Rose Med.						#642	#392	Beige Grey Dk.					#3047	#852	Yellow Beige Lt.
			#367	#217	Pistachio Green Dk.						#644	#830	Beige Grey Lt.					#3053	#261	Pine Green Lt.
			#368	#214	Pistachio Green Lt.						#646	#8581	Beaver Grey Dk.					#3364	#260	Celery Green Lt.
			#369	#1043	Pistachio Green Pale						#745	#300	Topaz Very Lt.					#3712	#1023	Salmon Med.
			#420	#374	Hazel Nut Dk.						#760	#1022	Salmon					#3721	#896	Shell Pink Med. Dk.
			#422	#373	Hazel Nut Lt.						#761	#1021	Salmon Lt.					#3743	#869	Antique Violet Very Lt.
			#502	#877	Sage Green Med.						#819	#271	Antique Rose Pale					#3752	#1032	Blue Denim Very Lt.
			#522	#8860	Fern Green Med.						#950	#4146	Fawn					#3773	#1008	Rose Blush Dk.
			#524	#858	Fern Green Very Lt.						#3013	#842	Olive Green Lt.					#3813	#213	Sage Green Very Lt.
			#612	#832	Butternut Med.						#3041	#871	Antique Violet					White	#2	White
			#613	#831	Butternut						#3042	#870	Antique Violet Lt.							

Joe's
Poem

Joe's Poem

Designed by Christine A. Hendricks

Materials
- 13" x 16" piece of rose
  14-count Aida

Instructions
Center and stitch design, using two strands floss for Cross-Stitch and one strand floss for Backstitch and French Knot.

Stitch Count:
138 wide x 92 high

Approximate Design Size:
11-count 12⅝" x 8⅜"
14-count 9⅞" x 6⅝"
16-count 8⅝" x 5¾"
18-count 7¾" x 5⅛"
22-count 6⅜" x 4¼"

X	B'st	Fr	DMC	ANCHOR	COLORS	X	B'st	DMC	ANCHOR	COLORS
			#208	#110	Lavender Dk.		✎	#699	#923	Kelly Green Dk.
			#209	#109	Lavender Med.			#701	#227	Kelly Green Med.
•	✎	●	#310	#403	Black	+		#725	#305	Topaz Med.
△		●	#498	#1005	Garnet			#727	#293	Topaz Lt.
≷			#601	#57	Cranberry Dk.	S		#741	#304	Tangerine Dk.
			#603	#62	Cranberry			#799	#136	Blueberry Med.
O			#605	#50	Cranberry Very Lt.	V		#800	#144	Blueberry Pale

Make a joyful noise unto the Lord in all ye lands. Serve the Lord with gladness: come before his presence with singing.

Make a Joyful Noise

Designed by Kathleen Hurley

Materials
- 12" x 16" piece of potato 25-count Lugana®

Stitch Count:
124 wide x 78 high

Approximate Design Size:
11-count 11⅜" x 7⅛"
14-count 8⅞" x 5⅝"
16-count 7¾" x 4⅞"
18-count 7" x 4⅜"
22-count 5⅝" x 3⅝"
25-count over two
threads 10" x 6¼"

Instructions
Center and stitch design, stitching over two threads and using two strands floss for Cross-Stitch and one strand floss for Backstitch and French Knot.

Let your heart be glad in the knowledge of the Lord when you proclaim your faith with the radiant colors of Nature's grandeur stitched in bountiful blooms.

Hummingbird & Heart

Hummingbird & Heart

Designed by Kathleen Hurley

Materials
- 12" x 14" piece of lambswool 28-count Linen

Instructions

Center and stitch design, stitching over two threads and using two strands floss for Cross-Stitch and one strand floss for Backstitch, Straight Stitch and French Knot.

Stitch Count:
108 wide x 88 high

Approximate Design Size:
11-count 9⅞" x 8"
14-count 7¾" x 6⅜"
16-count 6¾" x 5½"
18-count 6" x 5"
22-count 5" x 4"
28-count over two threads 7¾" x 6⅜"

X	B'st	¼x	Str	Fr	DMC	ANCHOR	COLORS
★	✔	◪			#310	#403	Black
2		◪			#349	#13	Coral Dk.
⬕					#351	#10	Coral
T		◪			#562	#210	Jade Med.
●		◪			#563	#208	Jade Lt.
S		◪			#603	#62	Cranberry
◻		◪			#605	#50	Cranberry Very Lt.
◼		◻			#702	#226	Kelly Green Lt.
▲		◻			#704	#256	Parrot Green Med.
+		◻			#743	#302	Tangerine Lt.
▼		◻			#745	#300	Topaz Very Lt.
	✔				#791	#178	Darkest Cornflower Blue
O		◪			#793	#176	Cornflower Blue Lt.
◻		◻			#794	#175	Cornflower Blue Very Lt.
	✔		✔	◻	#801	#359	Coffee Brown Dk.
	✔				#895	#1044	Darkest Ivy Green
✳		◪			#947	#330	Burnt Orange
◻		◻			#971	#316	Pumpkin
⦚		◪			#3072	#847	Pearl Grey
▷		◪			#3347	#266	Ivy Green
◘		◪			#3348	#264	Apple Green
	✔				#3803	#69	Mauve Dk.
ø		◪			#3821	#305	Golden Wheat
◡	✔	◪	✔	●	#3829	#374	Old Gold Very Dk.
◻		◻			White	#2	White

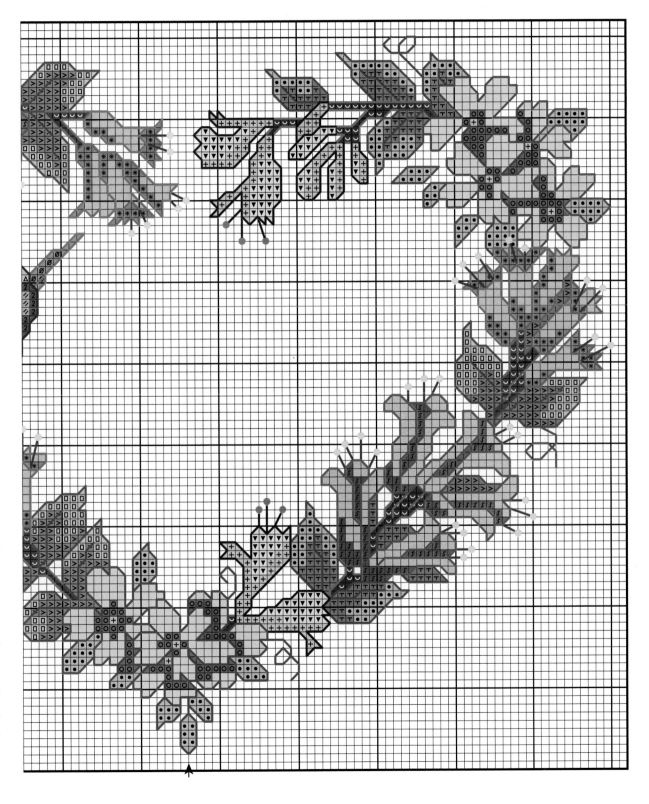

Feathers
& Flowers

Designed by Kathleen Hurley

Materials for One

- 9" x 13" piece of light blue 14-count Aida

Instructions

Center and stitch design of choice, using two strands floss for Cross-Stitch and one strand floss for Backstitch.

Sparrow
Stitch Count:
44 wide x 94 high

Approximate Design Size:
11-count 4" x 8⅝"
14-count 3¼" x 6¾"
16-count 2¾" x 5⅞"
18-count 2½" x 5¼"
22-count 2" x 4⅜"

Goldfinch
Stitch Count:
43 wide x 94 high

Approximate Design Size:
11-count 4" x 8⅝"
14-count 3⅛" x 6¾"
16-count 2¾" x 5⅞"
18-count 2⅜" x 5¼"
22-count 2" x 4⅜"

X	B'st	DMC	ANCHOR	COLORS
		#307	#289	Canary
★	✓	#310	#403	Black
		#413	#401	Charcoal
		#433	#358	Coffee Brown
		#435	#1046	Toast Dk.
		#700	#228	Kelly Green
•		#702	#226	Kelly Green Lt.
		#704	#256	Parrot Green Med.
		#738	#361	Toast Very Lt.
T		#741	#304	Tangerine Dk.
		#743	#302	Tangerine Lt.
O		#3607	#87	Plum
		#3608	#86	Plum Lt.
△		#3778	#1013	Terra Cotta
		White	#2	White

Sparrow

Goldfinch

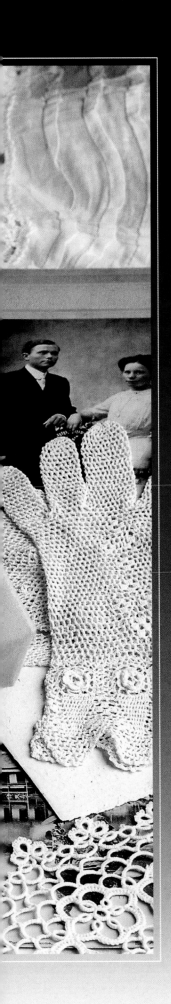

Country Flowers

Designed by P. A. Pearson

Materials

- 12" x 14" piece of white 25-count Dublin Linen
- 8" x 11½" fabric-covered box
- Mounting board
- 1 yd. twisted cord
- 1 yd. decorative trim
- Craft glue or glue gun

Stitch Count:
70 wide x 98 high

Approximate Design Size:
11-count 6⅜" x 9"
14-count 5" x 7"
16-count 4⅜" x 6⅛"
18-count 4" x 5½"
22-count 3¼" x 4½"
25-count over two
  threads 5⅝" x 7⅞"

Instructions

1: Center and stitch design, stitching over two threads and using two strands floss for Cross-Stitch and one strand floss for Backstitch. Tie two strands of black floss into a ¾" bow and sew to flower stems as shown in photo.

Note: From mounting board, cut one 6" x 8" piece.

2: Center and mount design over board. Position and glue mounted design to box as shown. Glue twisted cord, then decorative braid to box around outside edges of mounted design as shown.

Take a stroll down memory lane and recall kinder, gentler days when you stitch this elegantly old-fashioned keepsake box to safeguard your mementos.

X	B'st	DMC	ANCHOR	COLORS	X	B'st	DMC	ANCHOR	COLORS	X	DMC	ANCHOR	COLORS
S		#300	#352	Mahogany Very Dk.			#718	#88	Plum Med.		#814	#45	Garnet Very Dk.
		#301	#1049	Cinnamon Lt.	N		#745	#300	Topaz Very Lt.	•	#822	#390	Beige Grey Very Lt.
	✓	#310	#403	Black	★		#781	#309	Russet Med.		#828	#158	Larkspur Lt.
		#498	#1005	Garnet	O		#782	#308	Russet		#915	#1029	Plum Very Dk.
		#702	#226	Kelly Green Lt.	T		#783	#307	Topaz Very Dk.	V	#937	#268	Black Avocado
⤨		#703	#238	Parrot Green		✓	#796	#133	Royal Blue	△	#3325	#129	Delft Blue
≡		#712	#926	Cream Very Pale	Ø		#798	#131	Blueberry Dk.		#3820	#306	Golden Wheat Dk.

Birdhouse

Birdhouse

Designed by Mike Vickery

Materials
- 13" x 13" piece of white 14-count Aida

Instructions
Center and stitch design, using two strands floss for Cross-Stitch and one strand floss for Backstitch.

Stitch Count:
95 wide x 100 high

Approximate Design Size:
11-count 8⅝" x 9⅛"
14-count 6⅞" x 7¼"
16-count 6" x 6¼"
18-count 5⅜" x 5⅝"
22-count 4⅜" x 4⅝"

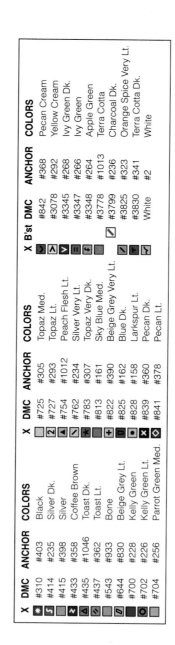

X	DMC	ANCHOR	COLORS
✳	#310	#403	Black
	#414	#235	Silver Dk.
	#415	#398	Silver
	#433	#358	Coffee Brown
	#435	#1046	Toast Dk.
	#437	#362	Toast Lt.
	#543	#933	Bone
	#644	#830	Beige Grey Lt.
	#700	#228	Kelly Green
	#702	#226	Kelly Green Lt.
◇	#704	#256	Parrot Green Med.

X	DMC	ANCHOR	COLORS
	#725	#305	Topaz Med.
2	#727	#293	Topaz Lt.
	#754	#1012	Peach Flesh Lt.
	#762	#234	Silver Very Lt.
✳	#783	#307	Topaz Very Dk.
	#813	#161	Sky Blue Med.
+	#822	#390	Beige Grey Very Lt.
▣	#825	#162	Blue Dk.
●	#828	#158	Larkspur Lt.
✕	#839	#360	Pecan Dk.
◇	#841	#378	Pecan Lt.

X	B'st	DMC	ANCHOR	COLORS
▶		#842	#368	Pecan Cream
∧		#3078	#292	Yellow Cream
⟩		#3345	#268	Ivy Green Dk.
∥		#3347	#266	Ivy Green
☐		#3348	#264	Apple Green
	◩	#3778	#1013	Terra Cotta
◥		#3799	#236	Charcoal Dk.
∥		#3825	#323	Orange Spice Very Lt.
⌐		#3830	#341	Terra Cotta Dk.
Y		White	#2	White

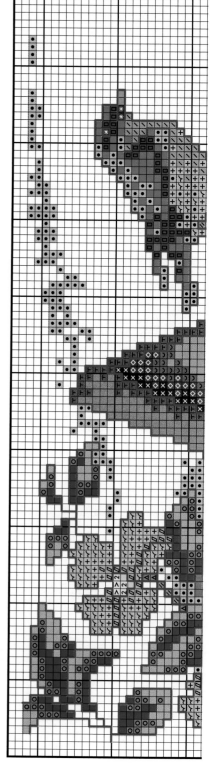

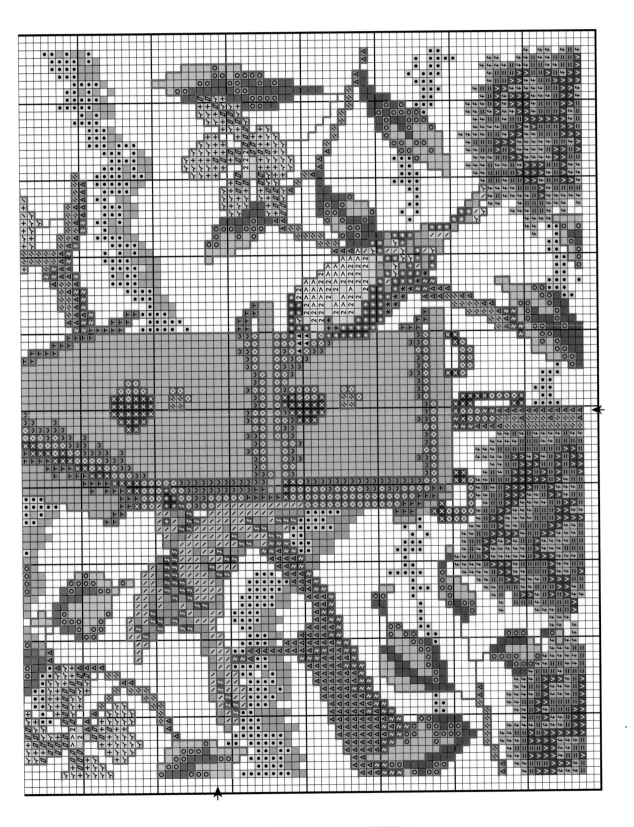

Stitch a bouquet of pint-sized flowers and a pleasant phrase for someone you love to send a heartfelt message as a reminder of life's endless blessings.

Sweet Peas

Designed by Felicia L. Williams

Materials

- 10" x 12" piece of ivory 14-count Aida
- Basket of choice
- Lightweight cardboard
- ¾ yd. gathered lace
- ¾ yd. pearl bead string
- Craft glue or glue gun

Instructions

1: Center and stitch design, using two strands floss for Cross-Stitch and one strand floss for Backstitch. Use one strand coordinating floss for securing beads.

Note: From lightweight cardboard, cut one 5¼" x 6⅞" piece.

2: Center and mount design over cardboard. Glue lace to back outside edges of mounted design. Glue pearl bead string around outside edges of mounted design. Position and glue mounted design to front of basket as shown in photo.

Stitch Count:
82 wide x 61 high

Approximate Design Size:
11-count 7½" x 5⅝"
14-count 5⅞" x 4⅜"
16-count 5⅛" x 3⅞"
18-count 4⅝" x 3⅜"
22-count 3¾" x 2⅞"

X	B'st	¼x	DMC	ANCHOR	COLORS
			#208	#110	Lavender Dk.
			#210	#108	Lavender Lt.
			#211	#342	Lavender Pale
			#310	#403	Black
			#469	#267	Avocado Green Med.
			#471	#266	Avocado Green Very Lt.
			#601	#57	Cranberry Dk.
			#603	#62	Cranberry
			#605	#50	Cranberry Very Lt.
			#676	#891	Honey
			#744	#301	Tangerine Pale
			#746	#275	Honey Pale
			#797	#132	Deep Blueberry
			#799	#136	Blueberry Med.
			#800	#144	Blueberry Pale

SEED BEADS

●	#00561	Ice Green

Chapter Two

Spread good cheer as an
angel on wing, touching a heart,
lifting a soul, stitching a
chuckle not yet born.

Country Humor

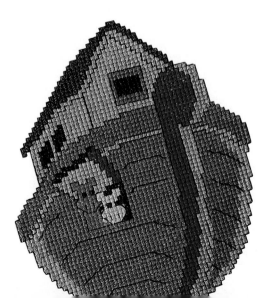

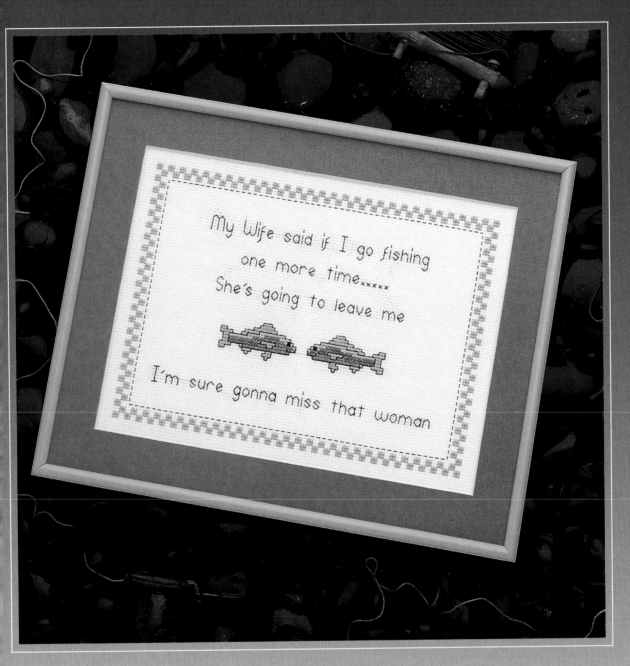

My Wife said if I go fishing
one more time.....
She's going to leave me

I'm sure gonna miss that woman

Tickle mute canvas with needle and thread,
'til its peals of laughter burst forth as a witty
prescription for smiles galore.

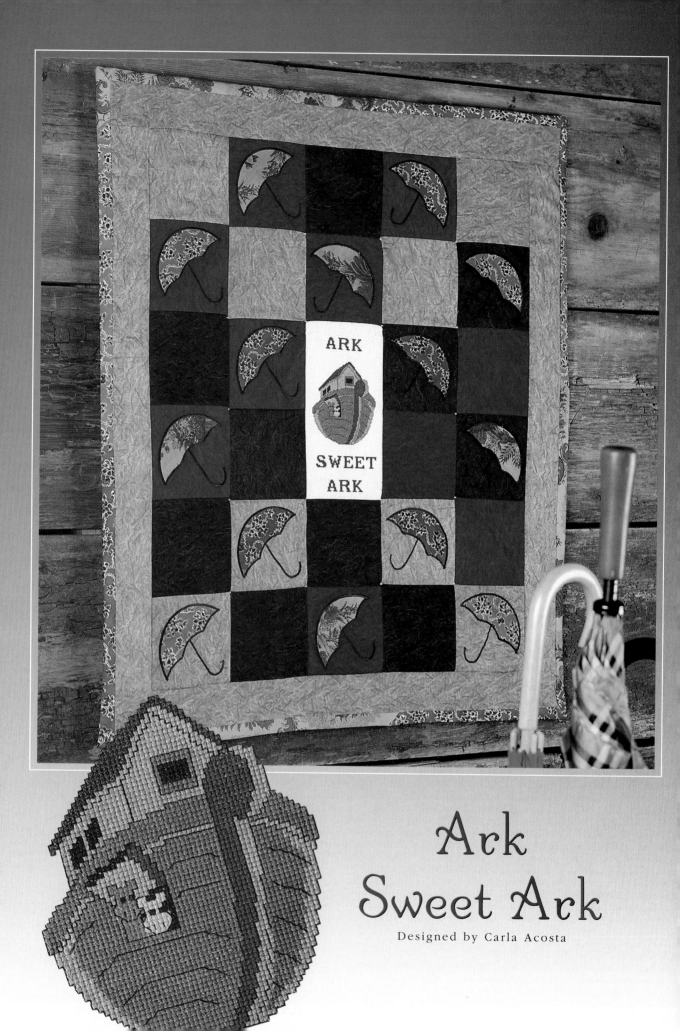

Ark
Sweet Ark

Designed by Carla Acosta

Materials
- 10" x 14" piece of ivory 16-count Aida
- ¾ yd. fabric #1
- ¾ yd. fabric #2
- ¾ yd. fabric #3
- 2 yds. fabric #4
- ½ yd. fabric #5
- ½ yd. fabric #6
- Batting

Instructions
1: Center and stitch design, using two strands floss for Cross-Stitch and one strand floss for Backstitch.

Notes: Trim design to 5½" x 10". From fabric #1, cut five pieces according to Umbrella Pattern and three 3" x 17" bias strips. From fabric #2, cut five pieces according to Umbrella Pattern and three 3" x 17" bias strips. From fabric #3, cut four pieces according to Umbrella Pattern and two 3" x 17" bias strips. From fabric #4, cut eight 5½" x 5½" for A pieces, two 3" x 28" for D pieces, two 3¼" x 28" for E pieces and one 28" x 32" piece for back. From fabric #5, cut ten 5½" x 5½" for B pieces and from fabric #6, cut ten 5½" x 5½" for C pieces. From batting, cut one 28" x 32" piece. Use ½" seam allowance.

2: For front, with right sides facing sew design, A, B, C, D and E pieces together according to Front Assembly Diagram.

3: Following Appliqué Pattern, sew umbrellas onto blocks as indicated on Appliqué Fabric Key and Appliqué Placement Diagram.

4: With wrong sides facing and batting between, baste front and back together, forming wall hanging. Sewing through all thicknesses, sew around inside edges of D and E pieces. Sewing through all thicknesses, tack wall hanging together at several fabric corners or as desired.

5: Alternating fabrics, sew short ends of bias strips together, forming binding. Press under ½" on each long edge of binding. With right sides facing, sew binding to front outside edges of wall hanging, folding corners as you sew. Fold binding to back and slip stitch in place. Hang as desired.

Appliqué Pattern

Umbrella Pattern

Appliqué Fabric Key
- Fabric #1
- Fabric #2
- Fabric #3

Front Assembly Diagram

	D				
A	B	C	B	A	
B	A	B	A	C	
C	B	ARK	C	B	
B	C	SWEET ARK	B	C	
C	A	C	A	B	
A	C	B	C	A	
	D				

E ... E

Appliqué Placement Diagram

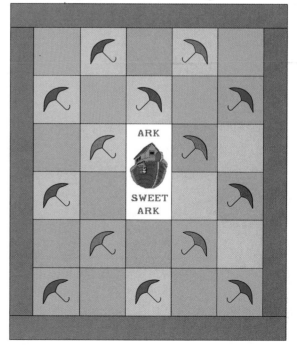

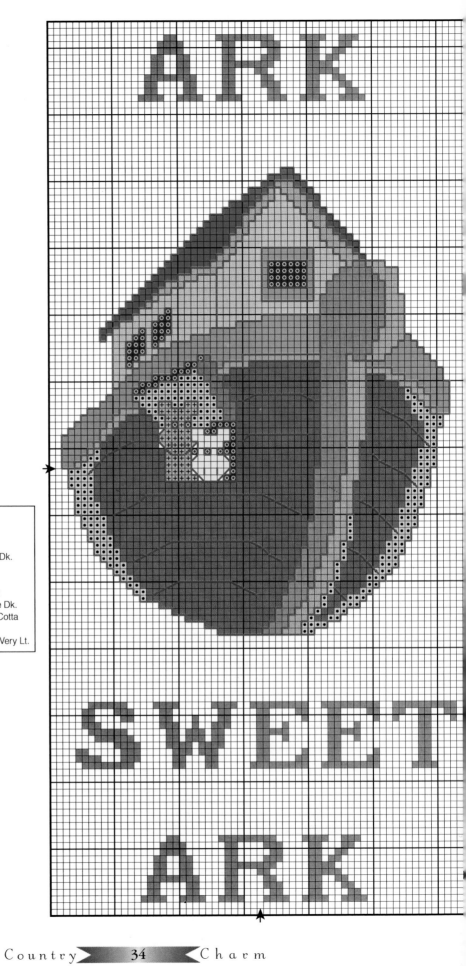

Stitch Count:
61 wide x 130 high

Approximate Design Size:
11-count 5⅝" x 11⅞"
14-count 4⅜" x 9⅜"
16-count 3⅞" x 8⅛"
18-count 3⅜" x 7¼"
22-count 2⅞" x 6"

X	B'st	¼x	DMC	ANCHOR	COLORS
■			#434	#310	Darkest Toast
⊡			#436	#1045	Toast
✚		◪	#720	#326	Orange Spice Dk.
■			#890	#218	Spruce Dk.
▫			#3347	#266	Ivy Green
◉		◪	#3371	#382	Darkest Brown
▨			#3726	#1018	Antique Mauve Dk.
▨			#3777	#1015	Darkest Terra Cotta
▨			#3778	#1013	Terra Cotta
▫		◪	#3825	#323	Orange Spice Very Lt.

I Collect
Angels

I Collect Angels

Designed by Carla Acosta

Materials
- 14" x 14" piece of oatmeal 14-count Fiddler's Cloth

Instructions
Center and stitch design, using two strands floss for Cross-Stitch and one strand floss for Backstitch and Running Stitch.

Stitch Count:
117 wide x 107 high

Approximate Design Size:
11-count 10⅝" x 9¾"
14-count 8⅜" x 7¾"
16-count 7⅜" x 6¾"
18-count 6½" x 6"
22-count 5⅜" x 4⅞"

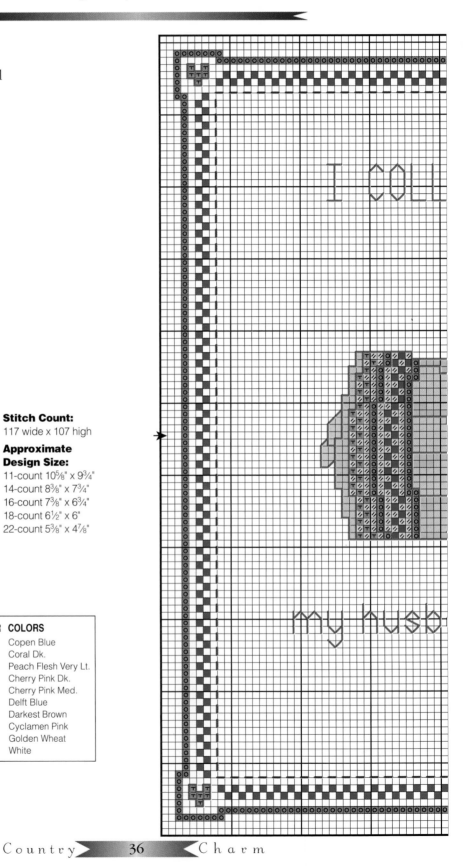

X	B'st	¼x	Run	DMC	ANCHOR	COLORS
■				#322	#978	Copen Blue
⊤				#349	#13	Coral Dk.
□		▨		#948	#1011	Peach Flesh Very Lt.
□				#956	#40	Cherry Pink Dk.
□				#957	#50	Cherry Pink Med.
△				#3325	#129	Delft Blue
●	▨		▨	#3371	#382	Darkest Brown
◉				#3805	#62	Cyclamen Pink
□				#3821	#305	Golden Wheat
▨				White	#2	White

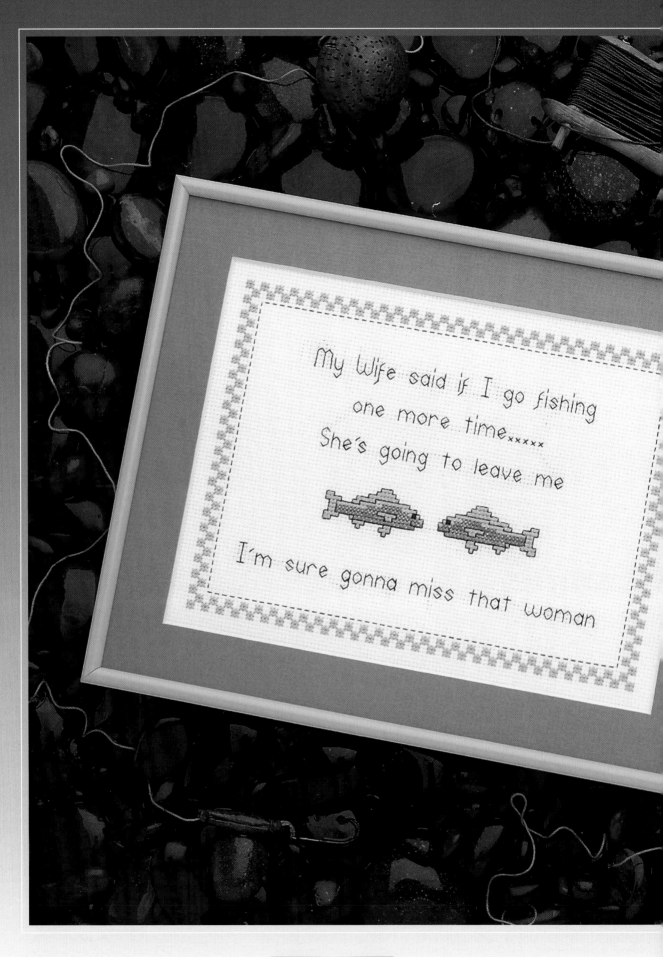

My wife said if I go fishing
one more time.....
She's going to leave me

I'm sure gonna miss that woman

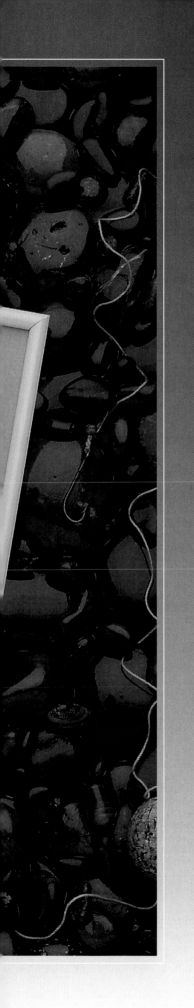

My Wife Said

Designed by Carla Acosta

Materials
- 12" x 15" piece of antique white 14-count Aida

Instructions
Center and stitch design, using two strands floss for Cross-Stitch and one strand floss for Backstitch and Running Stitch.

Stitch Count:
118 wide x 86 high

Approximate Design Size:
11-count 10¾" x 7⅞"
14-count 8½" x 6¼"
16-count 7⅜" x 5⅜"
18-count 6⅝" x 4⅞"
22-count 5⅜" x 4"

Watch them take the bait, then reel in humor from a different angle with this tongue-in-cheek sampler designed to catch every fisherman's fancy.

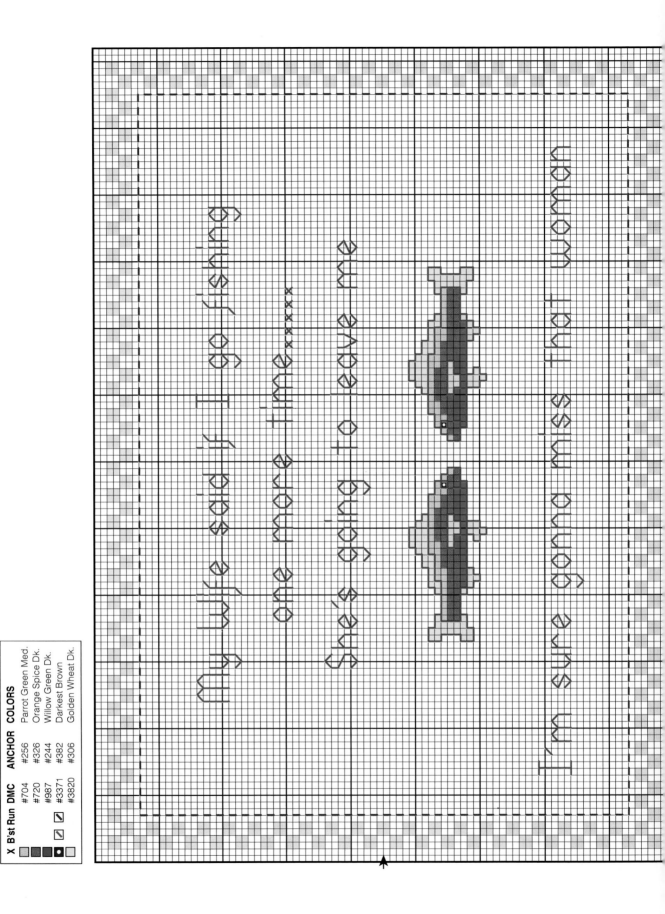

My wife said I go fishing
one more time××××××
She's going to leave me

I'm sure gonna miss that woman

X	B'st Run	DMC	ANCHOR	COLORS
		#704	#256	Parrot Green Med.
		#720	#326	Orange Spice Dk.
		#987	#244	Willow Green Dk.
		#3371	#382	Darkest Brown
		#3820	#306	Golden Wheat Dk.

CAUTION

DUST BUNNY CROSSING

Caution, Dust Bunny

Caution, Dust Bunny

Designed by Carla Acosta

Materials

- 13" x 14" piece of white 14-count Aida

Instructions

Center and stitch design, using two strands floss for Cross-Stitch and one strand floss for Backstitch and Running Stitch.

Stitch Count:
112 wide x 97 high

Approximate Design Size:
11-count 10¼" x 8⅞"
14-count 8" x 7"
16-count 7" x 6⅛"
18-count 6¼" x 5⅜"
22-count 5⅛" x 4½"

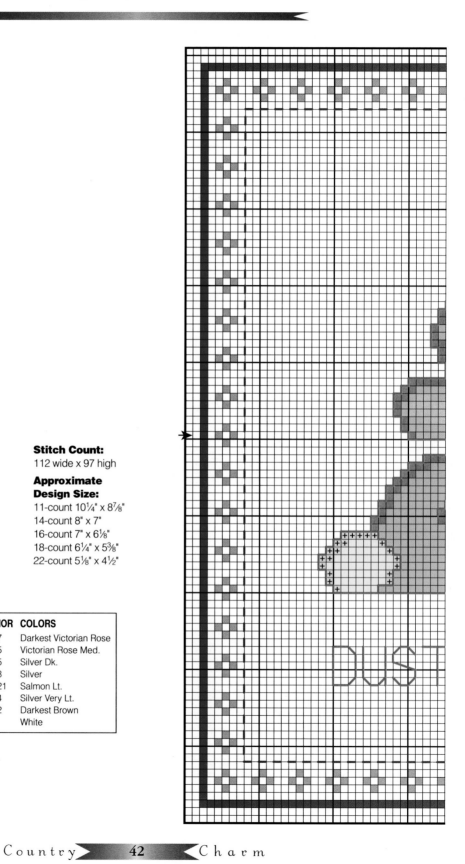

X	B'st	Run	DMC	ANCHOR	COLORS
■			#221	#897	Darkest Victorian Rose
▨			#223	#895	Victorian Rose Med.
▨			#414	#235	Silver Dk.
▨			#415	#398	Silver
▨			#761	#1021	Salmon Lt.
⊞			#762	#234	Silver Very Lt.
◨	◪	◪	#3371	#382	Darkest Brown
□			White	#2	White

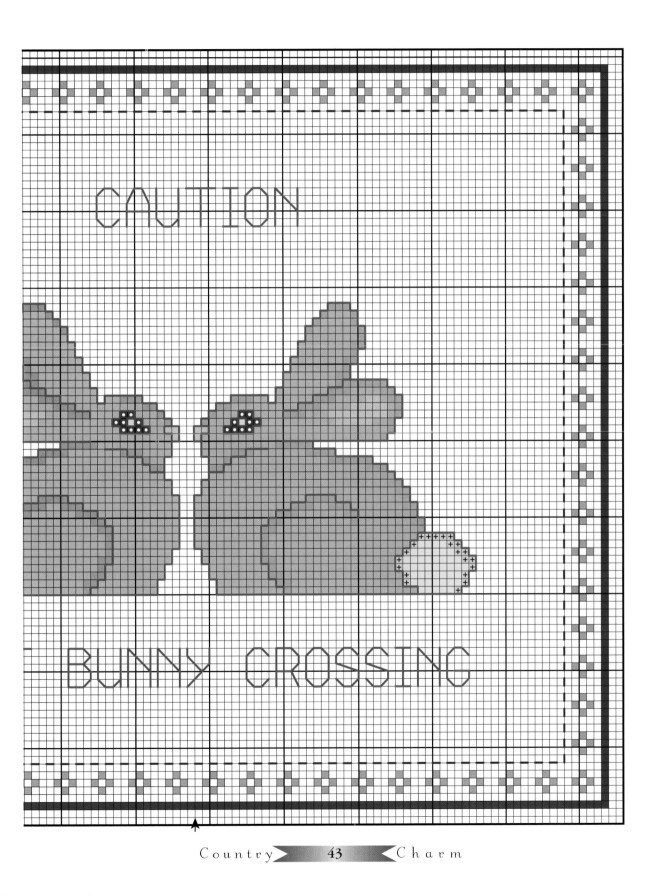

When I prayed for patience... God gave me children.

Strewn with vivid imagery depicting the joys of parenthood, this witty plaque serves as a whimsical reminder that our children are too soon grown.

When I Prayed

Designed by Christine A. Hendricks

Materials

• 10" x 13" piece of light blue 14-count Aida

Instructions

Center and stitch design, using two strands floss for Cross-Stitch and one strand floss for Backstitch and French Knot.

Stitch Count:
98 wide x 51 high

Approximate Design Size:
11-count 9" x 4⅝"
14-count 7" x 3¾"
16-count 6⅛" x 3¼"
18-count 5½" x 2⅞"
22-count 4½" x 2⅜"

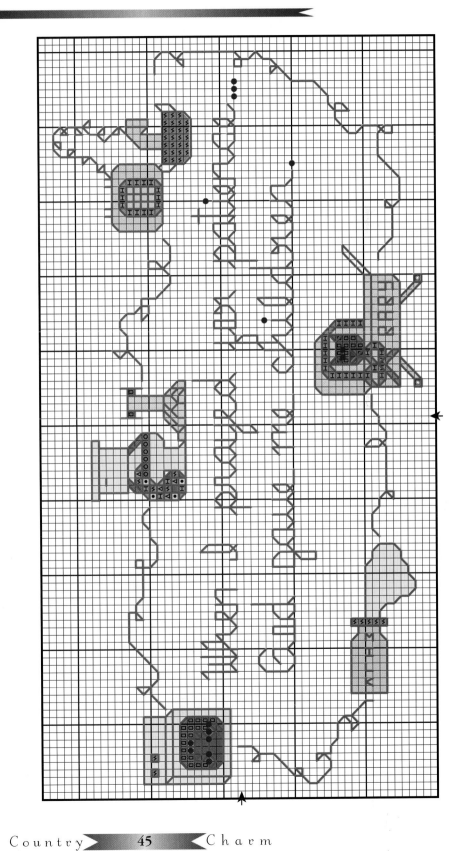

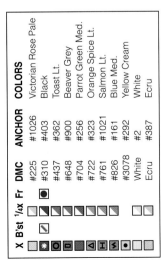

X	B'st	¼x	Fr	DMC	ANCHOR	COLORS
			●	#225	#1026	Victorian Rose Pale
				#310	#403	Black
				#437	#362	Toast Lt.
				#648	#900	Beaver Grey
				#704	#256	Parrot Green Med.
				#722	#323	Orange Spice Lt.
				#761	#1021	Salmon Lt.
				#826	#161	Blue Med.
				#3078	#292	Yellow Cream
				White	#2	White
				Ecru	#387	Ecru

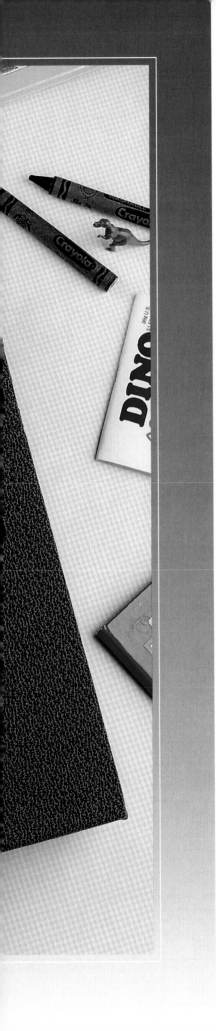

Dino-Mite

Designed by Gina Graham

Materials for One
- 11" x 11" piece of bisque 14-count Aida
- 1 yd. of fabric
- ⅓ yd. contrasting fabric

Instructions

1: Select desired letters for name from Alphabet graph, center and stitch design of choice, using two strands floss for Cross-Stitch and one strand floss for Backstitch and French Knot.

Notes: Trim "Luke" design to 6⅛" x 6⅞" or "Nathan" design to 6⅞" x 6⅞". From fabric, cut four 16" x 16" pieces for front, back, and front and back lining pieces. From contrasting fabric, cut one 1" x 24" piece for trim and two 3" x 22" pieces for handles. Use ½" seam allowance.

2: Press under ½" on side and bottom edges of design. Fold trim in half lengthwise; press. Baste trim to side and bottom edges of design.

Press under ½" on top edge of design, forming pocket. Position and sew side and bottom edges of pocket to front piece as shown in photo.

3: With right sides facing, sew front and back together at sides and bottom; form corners following Corner Illustration, forming tote. Turn right sides out. Repeat with lining front and back pieces, forming lining.

4: With right sides facing, sew tote and lining together around top edge, leaving an opening for turning. Turn right sides out; slip stitch opening closed.

5: For handles, with right sides facing, fold each piece in half lengthwise, sew long edges together. Turn right sides out; press. Position and sew one handle to front and one handle to back at top inside edges of tote as shown in photo.

Alphabet

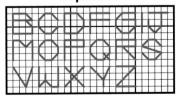

Corner Illustration

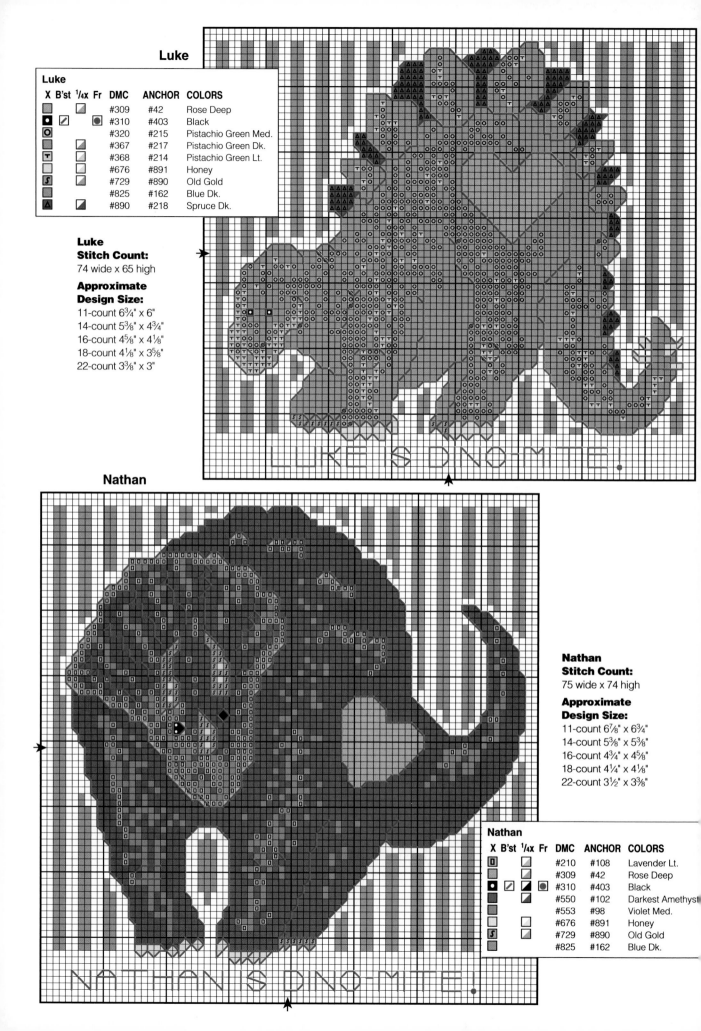

Luke

Luke

X	B'st	1/4x	Fr	DMC	ANCHOR	COLORS
				#309	#42	Rose Deep
				#310	#403	Black
				#320	#215	Pistachio Green Med.
				#367	#217	Pistachio Green Dk.
				#368	#214	Pistachio Green Lt.
				#676	#891	Honey
				#729	#890	Old Gold
				#825	#162	Blue Dk.
				#890	#218	Spruce Dk.

Luke
Stitch Count:
74 wide x 65 high

Approximate
Design Size:
11-count 6¾" x 6"
14-count 5⅜" x 4¾"
16-count 4⅝" x 4⅛"
18-count 4⅛" x 3⅝"
22-count 3⅜" x 3"

Nathan

Nathan
Stitch Count:
75 wide x 74 high

Approximate
Design Size:
11-count 6⅞" x 6¾"
14-count 5⅜" x 5⅜"
16-count 4¾" x 4⅝"
18-count 4¼" x 4⅛"
22-count 3½" x 3⅜"

Nathan

X	B'st	1/4x	Fr	DMC	ANCHOR	COLORS
				#210	#108	Lavender Lt.
				#309	#42	Rose Deep
				#310	#403	Black
				#550	#102	Darkest Amethyst
				#553	#98	Violet Med.
				#676	#891	Honey
				#729	#890	Old Gold
				#825	#162	Blue Dk.

Witty
Kitties

Witty Kitties

Designed by Christine A. Hendricks

Materials
- 10" x 12" piece of honey suckle pink 16-count Aida
- One 10" x 12" piece and one 11" x 12" piece of white 14-count Aida
- Mounting board
- 2 yds. piping
- Lightweight cardboard
- Six 1" self-adhesive

magnet strips
- Craft glue or glue gun

Instructions

1: Center and stitch "Curiosity" design onto 10" x 12" piece of honeysuckle pink Aida; "Fe-Line" design onto 10" x 12" piece of white Aida; and "Sleeping" design onto 11" x 12" piece of white Aida, using two strands floss for Cross-Stitch and one strand floss for Backstitch, Straight Stitch and French Knot.

Notes: From mounting board, cut one 3½" x 5½" piece for "Curiosity"; one 3¾" x 6" piece for "Fe-Line"; and one 5" x 6" piece for "Sleeping." From piping, cut one 22" piece for "Curiosity"; one 24" piece for "Fe-Line"; and one 26" piece for "Sleeping." From lightweight cardboard, cut one 3" x 5" piece for "Curiosity"; one 3¼" x 5½" piece for "Fe-Line"; and one 4½" x 5½" piece for "Sleeping."

2: For each design, center and mount design over mounting board. Glue piping to outside edges of mounted design. Glue cardboard to back of mounted design; secure two magnets to cardboard following manufacturer's instructions.

Curiosity

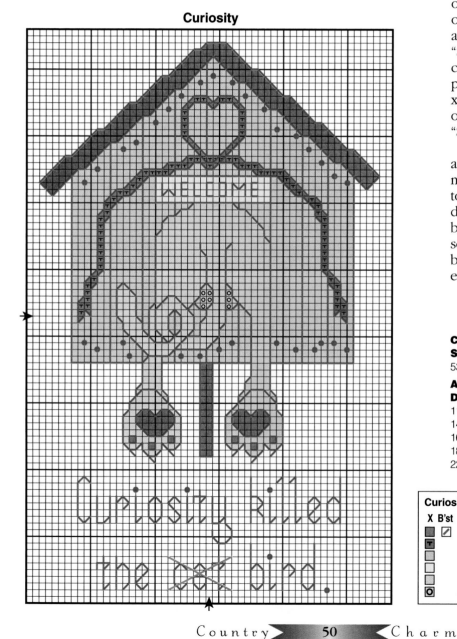

Curiosity
Stitch Count:
53 wide x 82 high

Approximate Design Size:
11-count 4⅞" x 7½"
14-count 3⅞" x 5⅞"
16-count 3⅜" x 5⅛"
18-count 3" x 4⅝"
22-count 2½" x 3¾"

Curiosity

X	B'st	¼x	Str	Fr	DMC	ANCHOR	COLORS
■	✓	◩	◩	●	#310	#403	Black
T	◩				#335	#38	Rose Pink Dk.
□	◩				#415	#398	Silver
□					#445	#288	Lemon Lt.
□					#899	#52	Rose Pink Med.
◉	◩				White	#2	White

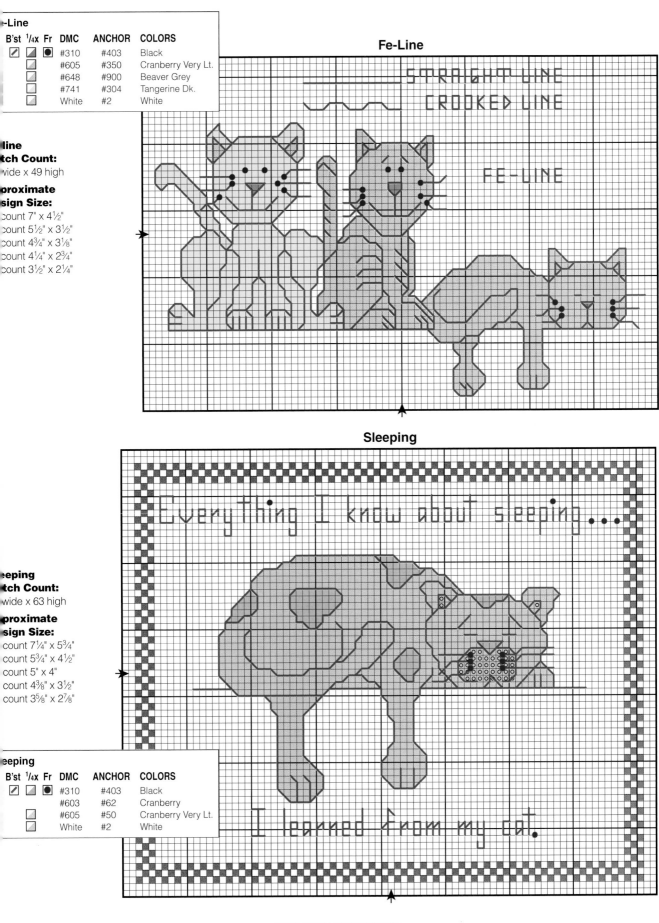

Fe-Line

STRAIGHT LINE
CROOKED LINE

FE-LINE

Fe-Line
Stitch Count:
wide x 49 high

Approximate
Design Size:
count 7" x 4½"
count 5½" x 3½"
count 4¾" x 3⅛"
count 4¼" x 2¾"
count 3½" x 2¼"

Sleeping

Everything I know about sleeping...

Sleeping
Stitch Count:
wide x 63 high

Approximate
Design Size:
count 7¼" x 5¾"
count 5¾" x 4½"
count 5" x 4"
count 4⅜" x 3½"
count 3⅝" x 2⅞"

I learned from my cat.

Chapter Three

Magic unfolds as strand
crosses strand, sculpting visions of
mystical realms, landscaped by
the fluid touch of a needleartist's hand.

Country Fantasy

Flitting fairies cast a precocious spell as stitch by stitch
they open the door ever wider, beckoning you
to enter their dreamy imagination land.

Fairies In Flowers

Designed by Phyllis Dobbs

Materials
- 13" x 13" piece of parchment 32-count Jobelan®
- ½ yd. fabric
- ¾ yd. contrasting fabric
- 1 yd. ⅛" cord
- 12" x 12" pillow form

Instructions

1: Center and stitch design, stitching over two threads and using two strands floss for Cross-Stitch and one strand floss for Backstitch.

Notes: Trim design to 8" x 8". From fabric, cut two 3¾" x 8" for A pieces, two 3¾" x 13½" for B pieces and two 9" x 13½" pieces for back. From contrasting fabric, cut one 1" x 36" bias strip for piping and one 5" x 108" piece for ruffle (piecing is necessary). Use ½" seam allowance.

2: Fold bias strip in half lengthwise with wrong sides facing and cord between; sew close to cord, forming piping.

3: With right sides facing, sew piping to design. With right sides facing, sew design, A and B pieces together according to Front Assembly Diagram, forming front.

4: For ruffle, with right sides facing, sew short ends of fabric together, forming ring. Fold wrong sides together; press. Gather unfinished edges to fit around outside edges of front; baste.

5: Hem one 13½" edge of each back piece. Place one hemmed edge over the other, overlapping enough to create a 13½" x 13½" back with opening. Baste outside edges together, press.

6: With right sides facing, sew front and back together. Trim seam and turn right sides out; press. Insert pillow form.

Front Assembly Diagram

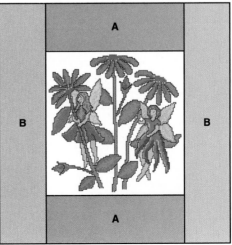

X	¼x	DMC	ANCHOR	COLORS
▨		#208	#110	Lavender Dk.
●		#209	#109	Lavender Med.
▢		#211	#342	Lavender Pale
▨	◪	#434	#310	Darkest Toast
T		#436	#1045	Toast
◿		#604	#55	Cranberry Lt.
>		#605	#50	Cranberry Very Lt.
V		#703	#238	Parrot Green
X		#743	#302	Tangerine Lt.
▢		#772	#259	Celery Green Very Lt.

X	B'st	¼x	¾x	DMC	ANCHOR	COLORS
▨			◪	#798	#131	Blueberry Dk.
▢				#800	#144	Blueberry Pale
◯				#809	#130	Blueberry Lt.
▨				#905	#257	Parrot Green Dk.
▢			▢	#945	#881	Blush
▤				#3348	#264	Apple Green
	◿			#3799	#236	Charcoal Dk.
▽				#3804	#63	Cyclamen Pink Dk.
▨				#3806	#76	Cyclamen Pink Lt.
			◪	White	#2	White

Stitch Count:
103 wide x 103 high

Approximate Design Size:
11-count 9⅜" x 9⅜"
14-count 7⅜" x 7⅜"
16-count 6½" x 6½"
18-count 5¾" x 5¾"
22-count 4¾" x 4¾"
32-count over two
threads 6½" x 6½"

Fairy
Reflections

Fairy Reflections

Designed by Phyllis Dobbs

Materials
- 12" x 15" piece of daffodil 14-count Damask Aida
- Wooden tray with 7¾" x 10¾" design opening

Instructions

Center and stitch design, using two strands floss for Cross-Stitch and one strand floss for Backstitch and French Knot. Position and secure design in tray following manufacturer's instructions.

Stitch Count:
119 wide x 86 high

Approximate Design Size:
11-count 10⅞" x 7⅞"
14-count 8½" x 6¼"
16-count 7½" x 5⅜"
18-count 6⅝" x 4⅞"
22-count 5½" x 4"

X	B'st	Fr	DMC	ANCHOR	COLORS
	✎		#310	#403	Black
●			#340	#118	Blue Violet
V			#341	#117	Blue Violet Lt.
			#367	#217	Pistachio Green Dk.
T			#368	#214	Pistachio Green Lt.
S			#369	#1043	Pistachio Green Pale
			#434	#310	Darkest Toast
╱			#436	#1045	Toast
			#552	#99	Violet Dk.
✕			#554	#96	Violet Lt.
∪			#605	#50	Cranberry Very Lt.
○			#702	#226	Kelly Green Lt.
			#704	#256	Parrot Green Med.
		◉	#743	#302	Tangerine Lt.
+			#745	#300	Topaz Very Lt.
			#799	#136	Blueberry Med.
			#800	#144	Blueberry Pale
☰			#917	#89	Plum Dk.
			#950	#4146	Fawn
>			#3607	#87	Plum
‖			#3608	#86	Plum Lt.
⇄			#3746	#1030	Blue Violet Med.
			White	#2	White

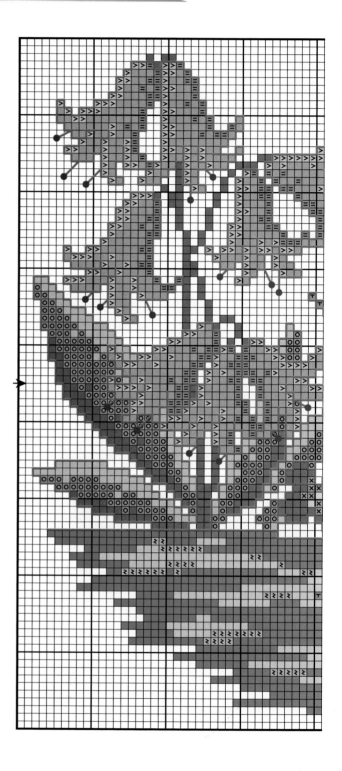

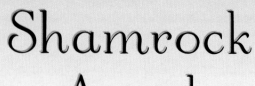

Shamrock Angel

Designed by P. A. Pearson

Materials

- 12" x 14" piece of white 25-count Lugana®

Instructions

Center and stitch design, stitching over two threads and using two strands floss, two strands blending filament or amounts indicated on color key for Cross-Stitch. Use one strand floss for Half Cross-Stitch, Backstitch and Straight Stitch.

Stitch Count:

70 wide x 97 high

Approximate Design Size:

11-count 6⅜" x 8⅞"
14-count 5" x 7"
16-count 4⅜" x 6⅛"
18-count 4" x 5⅜"
22-count 3¼" x 4½"
25-count over two
 threads 5⅝" x 7⅞"

X	½x	¼x	Str	DMC	ANCHOR	COLORS		X	B'st	Str	DMC	ANCHOR	KREINIK(BF)	COLORS
■	◪		◩	#436	#1045	Toast		●			#912	#209		Seafoam Green Dk.
◹				#437	#362	Toast Lt.					#913	#204		Seafoam
+		▨		#754	#1012	Peach Flesh Lt.					#948	#1011		Peach Flesh Very Lt.
✕				#776	#24	Rose Pink Lt.					#3326	#36		Rose Pink
■				#792	#941	Cornflower Blue Dk.		◹	◹		#3799	#236		Charcoal Dk.
▶				#818	#23	Antique Rose Very Lt.		▤			White	#2		White
▢				#819	#271	Antique Rose Pale		O			White	#2		White (one strand held with)
		▨		#827	#160	Sky Blue Lt.							#032	Pearl (one strand)
■		◹		#910	#229	Darkest Seafoam Green		T			Ecru	#387		Ecru
◡				#911	#205	Seafoam Green Very Dk.		▢					#032	Pearl

Silver Belle

Designed by Susan Stadler

Materials

- 15" x 16" piece of silver lurex 26-count Jobelan®
- Gift package ceramic button
- Antique silver toy soldier charm
- Three antique silver snowflake charms
- Ten silver 6mm jingle bells

Instructions

Center and stitch design, stitching over two threads and using three strands floss for Cross-Stitch and one strand floss for Backstitch. Use two strands floss or one strand ribbon for Straight Stitch. Attach button, charms and bells to design as shown in photo.

Envision the wonder of Christmas through the eyes of a child when you behold this enchanting carousel horse, magically arrayed in tinkling bells and shiny ribbon.

Stitch Count:
116 wide x 133 high

Approximate
Design Size:
11-count 10⅝" x 12⅛"
14-count 8⅜" x 9½"
16-count 7¼" x 8⅜"
18-count 6½" x 7⅜"
22-count 5⅜" x 6⅛"
26-count over two
   threads 9" x 10¼"

X	B'st	DMC	ANCHOR	COLORS	X	Str	DMC	ANCHOR	KREINIK(¹/₁₆)	WISPER	COLORS
		#310	#403	Black			#3021	#905			Brown Grey
		#317	#400	Darkest Silver			#3328	#1024			Salmon Dk.
		#321	#9046	Cherry Red			#3712	#1023			Salmon Med.
		#413	#401	Charcoal			#3727	#1016			Antique Mauve
		#415	#398	Silver			#3790	#393			Beige Grey Dk.
		#420	#374	Hazel Nut Dk.			#3799	#236			Charcoal
		#452	#232	Shell Grey Med.			#3801	#35			Geranium Med.
		#453	#231	Shell Grey Lt.			#3828	#888			Hazel Nut
		#814	#45	Garnet Very Dk.			#5283				Metallic Silver
		#815	#43	Garnet Dk.			#30745(Rayon)				Topaz Very Lt.
		#841	#378	Pecan Lt.			#35200(Rayon)				White
		#895	#1044	Darkest Ivy Green					#001HL		Silver Ribbon
		#987	#244	Willow Green Dk.						#60	Grey Heather
		#989	#242	Willow Green							

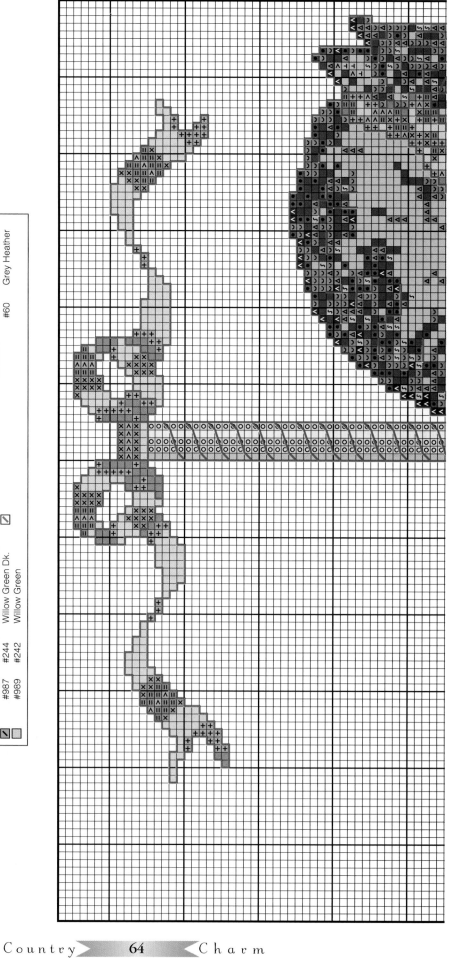

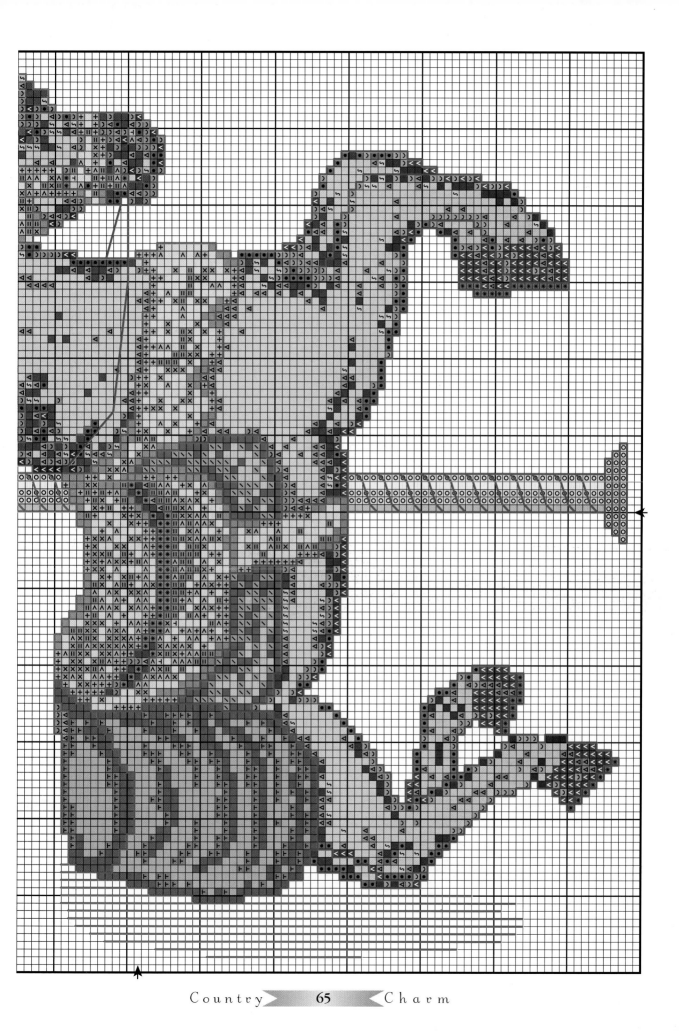

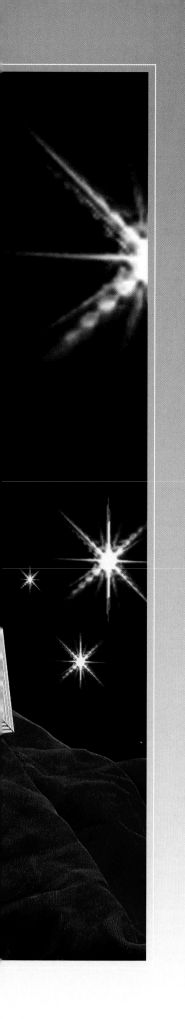

Angel Friends

Designed by Mike Vickery

Materials
- 14" x 16" piece of blueberry 22-count Janina

Instructions
Center and stitch design, stitching over two threads and using two strands floss or one strand very fine braid for Cross-Stitch. Use one strand floss for Backstitch.

Halcyon images of celestial companions evoke thoughts of the eternal beauty of friendship and the loving presence of our unseen heavenly guardians.

Stitch Count:

110 wide x 90 high

Approximate Design Size:

11-count 10" x 8¼"
14-count 7⅞" x 6½"
16-count 6⅞" x 5⅝"
18-count 6⅛" x 5"
22-count 5" x 4⅛"
22-count over two
  threads 10" x 8¼"

X	B'st	DMC	ANCHOR	KREINIK(#4)	COLORS
		#312	#979		Azure Blue Dk.
		#334	#977		Delft Blue Dk.
		#353	#8		Peach Flesh Med.
		#433	#358		Coffee Brown
		#435	#1046		Toast Dk.
		#601	#57		Cranberry Dk.
		#603	#62		Cranberry
		#604	#55		Cranberry Lt.
		#605	#50		Cranberry Very Lt.
		#644	#830		Beige Grey Lt.
		#725	#305		Topaz Med.
		#727	#293		Topaz Lt.
		#754	#1012		Peach Flesh Lt.
		#775	#128		Baby Blue
		#813	#161		Sky Blue Med.
		#822	#390		Beige Grey Very Lt.
		#825	#162		Blue Dk.
		#910	#229		Darkest Seafoam Green
		#912	#209		Seafoam Green Dk.
		#913	#204		Seafoam
		#948	#1011		Peach Flesh Very Lt.
		#955	#206		Seafoam Green Very Lt.
		#991	#189		Darkest Aquamarine
		#3325	#129		Delft Blue
		#3799	#236		Charcoal Dk.
				#002J	Gold
				#032	Pearl

Unicorn

Designed by Jason Williams

Materials
- 13" x 15" piece of gold/cream 14-count Aida

Instructions
Center and stitch design, using two strands floss for Cross-Stitch and one strand floss for Backstitch.

Stitch Count:
91 wide x 119 high

Approximate Design Size:
11-count 8⅜" x 10⅞"
14-count 6½" x 8½"
16-count 5¾" x 7½"
18-count 5⅛" x 6⅝"
22-count 4⅛" x 5½"

X	B'st	¼x	DMC	ANCHOR	COLORS
	✐		#310	#403	Black
			#336	#150	Indigo Blue
			#720	#326	Orange Spice Dk.
			#722	#323	Orange Spice Lt.
			#725	#305	Topaz Med.
			#939	#152	Navy Blue Ultra Very Dk.
			#3325	#129	Delft Blue
			#3807	#118	Cornflower Blue
			White	#2	White

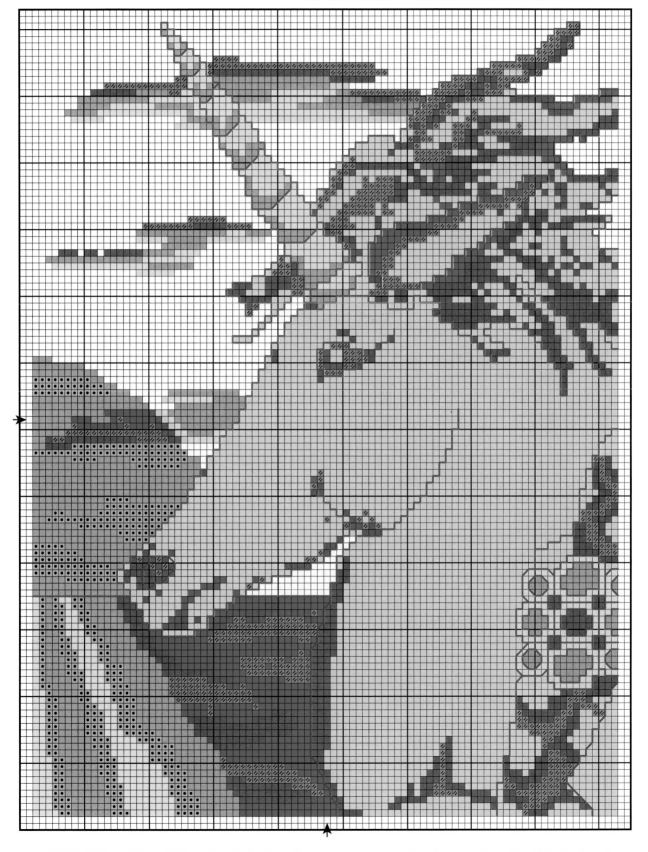

Angel Rose

Designed by Mike Vickery

Materials
- 15" x 16" piece of white 28-count Jubilee

Instructions
Center and stitch design, stitching over two threads and using two strands floss for Cross-Stitch and one strand floss for Backstitch.

Wrap yourself in peaceful dreams of an enchanted garden with this mesmerizing winged seraph, radiantly portrayed in a floral frame.

Stitch Count:

119 wide x 143 high

Approximate Design Size:

11-count 10⅞" x 13"
14-count 8½" x 10¼"
16-count 7½" x 9"
18-count 6⅝" x 8"
22-count 5½" x 6½"
28-count over two
  threads 8½" x 10¼"

X	DMC	ANCHOR	COLORS
	#319	#218	Spruce
	#320	#215	Pistachio Green Med.
	#335	#38	Rose Pink Dk.
	#352	#9	Peach Flesh Dk.
	#353	#8	Peach Flesh Med.
	#367	#217	Pistachio Green Dk.
	#368	#214	Pistachio Green Lt.
	#597	#168	Wedgewood Lt.
	#598	#167	Wedgewood Very Lt.
	#642	#392	Beige Grey Dk.
	#644	#830	Beige Grey Lt.
	#676	#891	Honey
	#677	#886	Honey Lt.
	#725	#305	Topaz Med.
	#727	#293	Topaz Lt.

X	B'st	DMC	ANCHOR	COLORS
		#776	#24	Rose Pink Lt.
		#783	#307	Topaz Very Dk.
		#818	#23	Antique Rose Very Lt.
		#822	#390	Beige Grey Very Lt.
		#899	#52	Rose Pink Med.
		#917	#89	Plum Dk.
		#948	#1011	Peach Flesh Very Lt.
		#3607	#87	Plum
		#3608	#86	Plum Lt.
		#3609	#85	Plum Very Lt.
	◿	#3799	#236	Charcoal Dk.
		#3809	#779	Wedgewood Med.
		#3811	#928	Wedgewood Very Pale
		White	#2	White

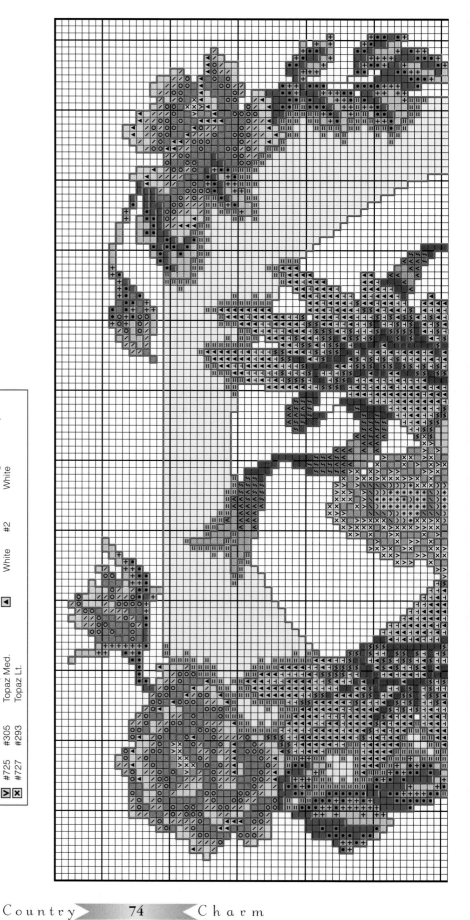

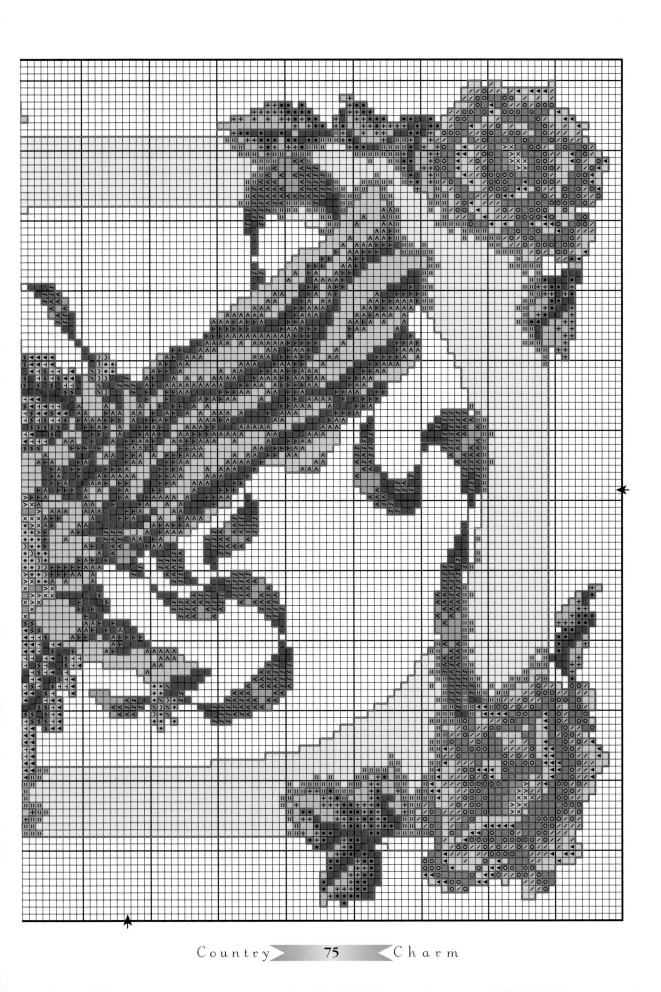

Chapter Four

A simple gift from the heart
made with canvas
and thread gives cause to remember
the reason for the season.

Country Christmas

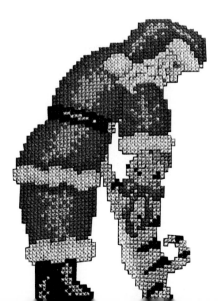

Decorated by slivers of silver and gold, bejeweled shades of
crimson and evergreen wrap themselves around your heart
to become treasured Christmas memories.

Artistically colorful and decidedly country, these quaint, loveable images help you capture the down-home flavor of the Yuletide season with a folk-art touch.

Christmas Folk Art

Designed by Phyllis Dobbs

Materials for One

- 16" x 16" piece of Christmas red (for "Angel") or Christmas green (for "Santa") 22-count Vienna
- ½ yd. fabric
- 1⅔ yds. piping
- 1⅔ yds. fringe (for "Angel")
- 1 yd. ribbon (for "Santa")
- 12" x 12" pillow form

Instructions

1: Center and stitch design of choice, stitching over two threads and using three strands floss for Cross-Stitch and one strand floss for Backstitch and French Knot.

Notes: Trim design to 13½" x 13½" for front. From fabric, cut two 9" x 13½" pieces for back. Use ½" seam allowance.

2: With right sides facing, sew piping to front; for

Santa

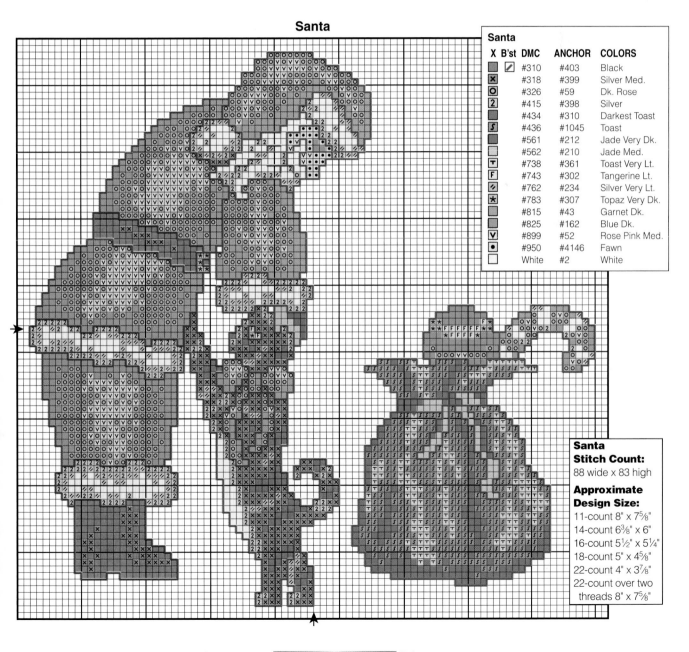

Santa

X	B'st	DMC	ANCHOR	COLORS
▨	✎	#310	#403	Black
✕		#318	#399	Silver Med.
○		#326	#59	Dk. Rose
2		#415	#398	Silver
▨		#434	#310	Darkest Toast
S		#436	#1045	Toast
▨		#561	#212	Jade Very Dk.
▨		#562	#210	Jade Med.
T		#738	#361	Toast Very Lt.
F		#743	#302	Tangerine Lt.
◪		#762	#234	Silver Very Lt.
✱		#783	#307	Topaz Very Dk.
▨		#815	#43	Garnet Dk.
▨		#825	#162	Blue Dk.
V		#899	#52	Rose Pink Med.
●		#950	#4146	Fawn
☐		White	#2	White

Santa Stitch Count:
88 wide x 83 high

Approximate Design Size:
11-count 8" x 7⅝"
14-count 6⅜" x 6"
16-count 5½" x 5¼"
18-count 5" x 4⅝"
22-count 4" x 3⅞"
22-count over two threads 8" x 7⅝"

"Angel," next sew fringe to front.

3: Hem one 13½" edge of each back piece. Place one hemmed edge over the other, overlapping enough to create a 13½" x 13½" back with opening. Baste outside edges together; press.

4: With right sides facing, sew front and back together. Trim seam and turn right sides out; press. For "Santa," tie ribbon into a bow and sew to front. Insert pillow form.

Angel
Stitch Count:
84 wide x 75 high

Approximate Design Size:
11-count 7⅝" x 6⅞"
14-count 6" x 5⅜"
16-count 5¼" x 4¾"
18-count 4¾" x 4¼"
22-count 3⅞" x 3½"
22-count over two
threads 7⅝" x 6⅞"

Angel

X	B'st	Fr	DMC	ANCHOR	COLORS
◪	✎		#310	#403	Black
K			#321	#9046	Cherry Red
▽			#415	#398	Silver
◼			#435	#1046	Toast Dk.
f			#437	#362	Toast Lt.
◼			#561	#212	Jade Very Dk.
●			#562	#210	Jade Med.
☐			#563	#208	Jade Lt.
◼			#666	#46	Geranium Dk.
+			#712	#926	Cream Very Pale
≷			#739	#387	Toast Pale
O			#743	#302	Tangerine Lt.
☆			#761	#1021	Salmon Lt.
2			#783	#307	Topaz Very Dk.
◼			#798	#131	Blueberry Dk.
☐			#948	#1011	Peach Flesh Very Lt.
✓			#3706	#33	Carnation Med.
◿		●	White	#2	White

Angel

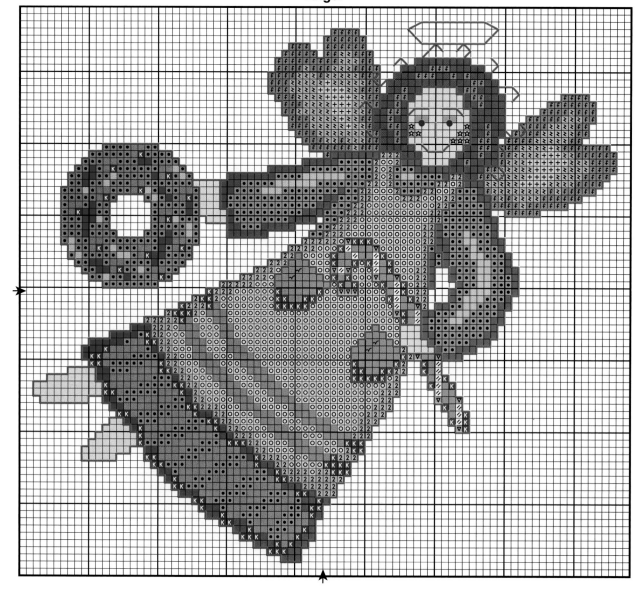

Joy to
the World

Joy to the World

Designed by Mike Vickery

Materials
- 12" x 18" piece of Amsterdam blue 28-count Pastel Linen

Instructions
Center and stitch design, stitching over two threads and using two strands floss for Cross-Stitch and one strand floss for Backstitch.

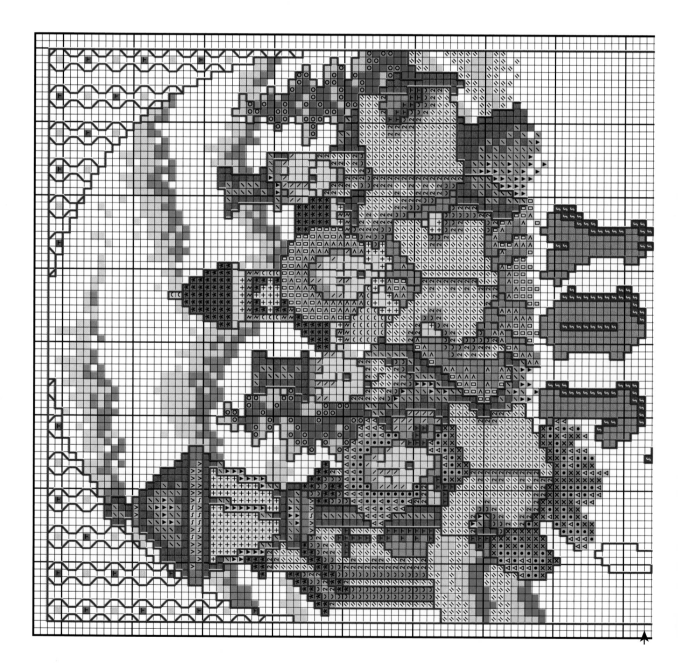

Stitch Count:
78 wide x 170 high

Approximate
Design Size:
11-count 7⅛" x 15½"
14-count 5⅝" x 12¼"
16-count 4⅞" x 10⅝"
18-count 4⅜" x 9½"
22-count 3⅝" x 7¾"
28-count over two
   threads 5⅝" x 12¼"

X	B'st	DMC	ANCHOR	COLORS
		#310	#403	Black
		#319	#218	Spruce
		#350	#11	Coral Med.
		#352	#9	Peach Flesh Dk.
		#353	#8	Peach Flesh Med.
		#356	#5975	Terra Cotta Med.
		#367	#217	Pistachio Green Dk.
		#368	#214	Pistachio Green Lt.
		#413	#401	Charcoal
		#414	#235	Silver Dk.
		#597	#168	Wedgewood Lt.
		#598	#167	Wedgewood Very Lt.
		#644	#830	Beige Grey Lt.
		#676	#891	Honey
		#677	#886	Honey Lt.
		#725	#305	Topaz Med.
		#727	#293	Topaz Lt.
		#746	#275	Honey Pale
		#758	#882	Terra Cotta Lt.
		#775	#128	Baby Blue
		#815	#43	Garnet Dk.
		#822	#390	Beige Grey Very Lt.
		#948	#1011	Peach Flesh Very Lt.
		#3325	#129	Delft Blue
		#3688	#66	Mauve
		#3689	#49	Mauve Very Lt.
		#3787	#393	Beige Grey Very Dk.
		#3799	#236	Charcoal Dk.
		#3803	#69	Mauve Dk.
		#3809	#779	Wedgewood Med.
		White	#2	White

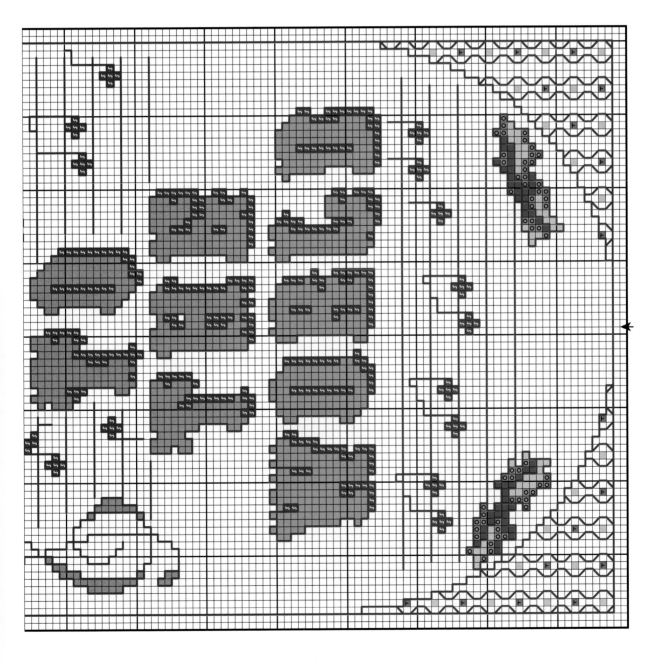

Christmas Montage

Designed by Mike Vickery

Materials
- 14" x 16" piece of ivory 14-count Damask Aida

Instructions
Center and stitch design, using two strands floss for Cross-Stitch and one strand floss for Backstitch.

Joyous memories of Christmases past flood your mind and warm your heart when you behold the colorful imagery depicted in this seasonal sampler.

Stitch Count:
144 wide x 105 high

**Approximate
Design Size:**
11-count 13⅛" x 9⅝"
14-count 10⅜" x 7½"
16-count 9" x 6⅝"
18-count 8" x 5⅞"
22-count 6⅝" x 4⅞"

X	B'st	DMC	ANCHOR	COLORS
△		#208	#110	Lavender Dk.
0		#210	#108	Lavender Lt.
⍿		#310	#403	Black
▨		#311	#148	Indigo Blue Dk.
☒		#322	#978	Copen Blue
▨		#350	#11	Coral Med.
T		#352	#9	Peach Flesh Dk.
▼		#353	#8	Peach Flesh Med.
+		#444	#290	Lemon Dk.
◪		#445	#288	Lemon Lt.
▨		#600	#59	Cranberry Very Dk.
∫		#602	#63	Cranberry Med.
⊟		#604	#55	Cranberry Lt.
⌣		#644	#830	Beige Grey Lt.
▨		#676	#891	Honey
⭕		#677	#886	Honey Lt.
■		#700	#228	Kelly Green
•		#702	#226	Kelly Green Lt.
☐		#704	#256	Parrot Green Med.
▼		#746	#275	Honey Pale
☐		#783	#307	Topaz Very Dk.
◣		#817	#13	Nasturtium
⊥		#822	#390	Beige Grey Very Lt.
☐		#948	#1011	Peach Flesh Very Lt.
☐		#3755	#140	Delft Blue Med.
	✓	#3799	#236	Charcoal Dk.
⇄		White	#2	White

Warm Winter Memories

Within the images:
SCATTER SEEDS OF FRIENDSHIP

Throughout your life, from day to day—

Remember the good times—
Let the bad melt away.

Warm Winter Memories

Designed by Christine A. Hendricks

Materials for One

- 10" x 13" piece of light blue 14-count Aida ("for Scatter Seeds of Friendship"); or 12" x 12" piece of white 14-count Aida (for "Let the Bad Melt Away"); or 12" x 14" piece of parchment 14-count Aida (for "Guardian Angel")
- Basket of choice
- Mounting board
- ¾ yd. piping (for "Scatter Seeds of Friendship")
- 1 yd. decorative trim (for "Guardian Angel")
- Desired amount of decorative trim and ribbon (for decorating basket of choice)
- Craft glue or glue gun

Instructions

1: Center and stitch design of choice, using two strands floss for Cross-Stitch and one strand floss for Backstitch and French Knot.

Note: From mounting board, cut one 4¼" x 7¼" piece for "Scatter Seeds of Friendship"; or one 6¼" x 6¼" piece for "Let the Bad Melt Away"; or one 5⅞" x 7¾" piece for "Guardian Angel."

2: Center and mount design over board. For "Scatter Seeds of Friendship," glue piping to back outside edges of mounted design. For "Guardian

Scatter Seeds of Friendship Stitch Count:
97 wide x 55 high

Approximate Design Size:
11-count 8⅞" x 5"
14-count 7" x 4"
16-count 6⅛" x 3½"
18-count 5⅜" x 3⅛"
22-count 4½" x 2½"

Scatter Seeds of Friendship

X	B'st	¼x	Fr	DMC	ANCHOR	COLORS
T	/	/	●	#310	#403	Black
✖		/		#322	#978	Copen Blue
		/		#334	#977	Delft Blue Dk.
		/		#415	#398	Silver
				#436	#1045	Toast
		/		#712	#926	Cream Very Pale
⊘				#726	#295	Topaz
●		/		#739	#387	Toast Pale
		/		#740	#316	Pumpkin Bright
		/		#911	#205	Seafoam Green Very Dk.
✳		/		#3705	#35	Carnation Dk.
O	/			#5283		Metallic Silver
△		/		White	#2	White

Scatter Seeds of Friendship

Angel," glue decorative trim to back outside edges of mounted design. Position and glue mounted design to front of basket as shown in photo.

3: Decorate basket with decorative trim and ribbon as shown or as desired.

Let the Bad Melt Away
Stitch Count:
85 wide x 87 high

Approximate Design Size:
11-count 7¾" x 8"
14-count 6⅛" x 6¼"
16-count 5⅜" x 5½"
18-count 4¾" x 4⅞"
22-count 3⅞" x 4"

Let the Bad Melt Away						
X	B'st	¼x	Fr	DMC	ANCHOR	COLORS
■	✓		●	#310	#403	Black
△				#606	#334	Bright Orange Red
□				#741	#304	Tangerine Dk.
▨		◪		#782	#308	Russet
□				#783	#307	Topaz Very Dk.
◎				#5283		Metallic Silver
□				White	#2	White

Let the Bad Melt Away

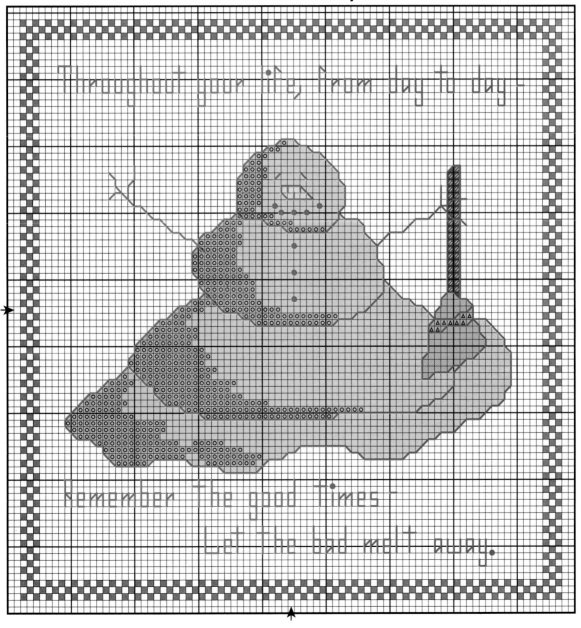

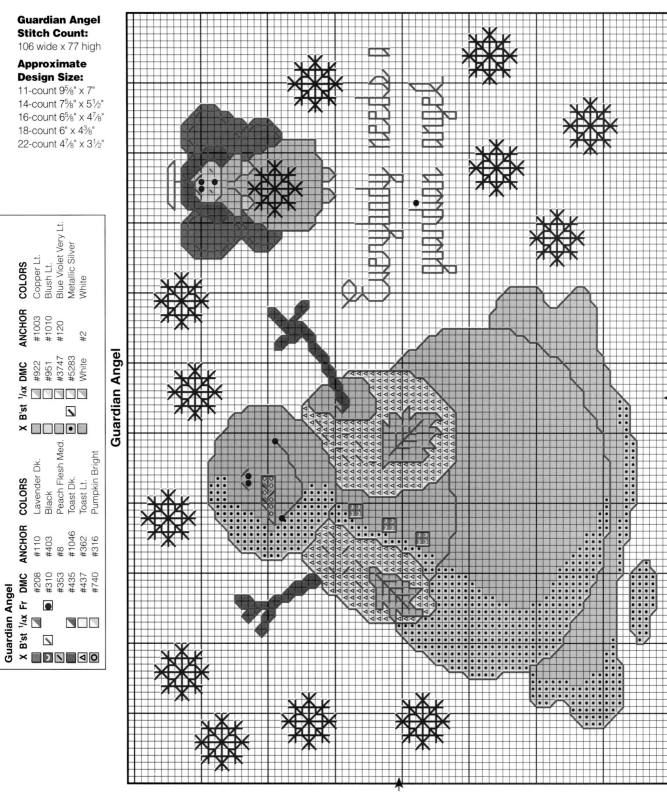

Guardian Angel Stitch Count:
106 wide x 77 high

Approximate Design Size:
11-count 9⅝" x 7"
14-count 7⅝" x 5½"
16-count 6⅝" x 4⅞"
18-count 6" x 4⅜"
22-count 4⅞" x 3½"

Guardian Angel

Guardian Angel

X	B'st	1/4x	DMC	ANCHOR	COLORS
			#922	#1003	Copper Lt.
			#951	#1010	Blush Lt.
			#3747	#120	Blue Violet Very Lt.
			#5283		Metallic Silver
			White	#2	White

Guardian Angel

X	B'st	1/4x	Fr	DMC	ANCHOR	COLORS
				#208	#110	Lavender Dk.
				#310	#403	Black
				#353	#8	Peach Flesh Med.
				#435	#1046	Toast Dk.
				#437	#362	Toast Lt.
				#740	#316	Pumpkin Bright

To everything there is a season

ABCDEFGHIJ
KLMNOPQRS
TUVWXYZ
0123456
789

All Seasons
Sampler

All Seasons Sampler

Designed by Felicia L. Williams

Materials

- 13" x 15" piece of antique white 14-count Aida

Instructions

Center and stitch design, using two strands floss for Cross-Stitch and one strand floss for Backstitch and French Knot.

Stitch Count:
94 wide x 126 high

Approximate Design Size:
11-count 8⅝" x 11½"
14-count 6¾" x 9"
16-count 5⅞" x 7⅞"
18-count 5¼" x 7"
22-count 4⅜" x 5¾"

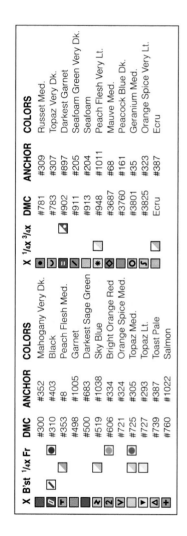

X	B'st	1/4x	Fr	DMC	ANCHOR	COLORS
■				#300	#352	Mahogany Very Dk.
■	■		●	#310	#403	Black
■		■		#353	#8	Peach Flesh Med.
■				#498	#1005	Garnet
■				#500	#683	Darkest Sage Green
■		■		#519	#1038	Sky Blue
■			●	#606	#334	Bright Orange Red
■				#721	#324	Orange Spice Med.
■		■	●	#725	#305	Topaz Med.
■		■		#727	#293	Topaz Lt.
■				#739	#387	Toast Pale
■				#760	#1022	Salmon

X	1/4x	3/4x	DMC	ANCHOR	COLORS
■			#781	#309	Russet Med.
■			#783	#307	Topaz Very Dk.
■		■	#902	#897	Darkest Garnet
■			#911	#205	Seafoam Green Very Dk.
■			#913	#204	Seafoam
■	■		#948	#1011	Peach Flesh Very Lt.
■			#3687	#68	Mauve Med.
■			#3760	#161	Peacock Blue Dk.
■			#3801	#35	Geranium Med.
■			#3825	#323	Orange Spice Very Lt.
■	■		Ecru	#387	Ecru

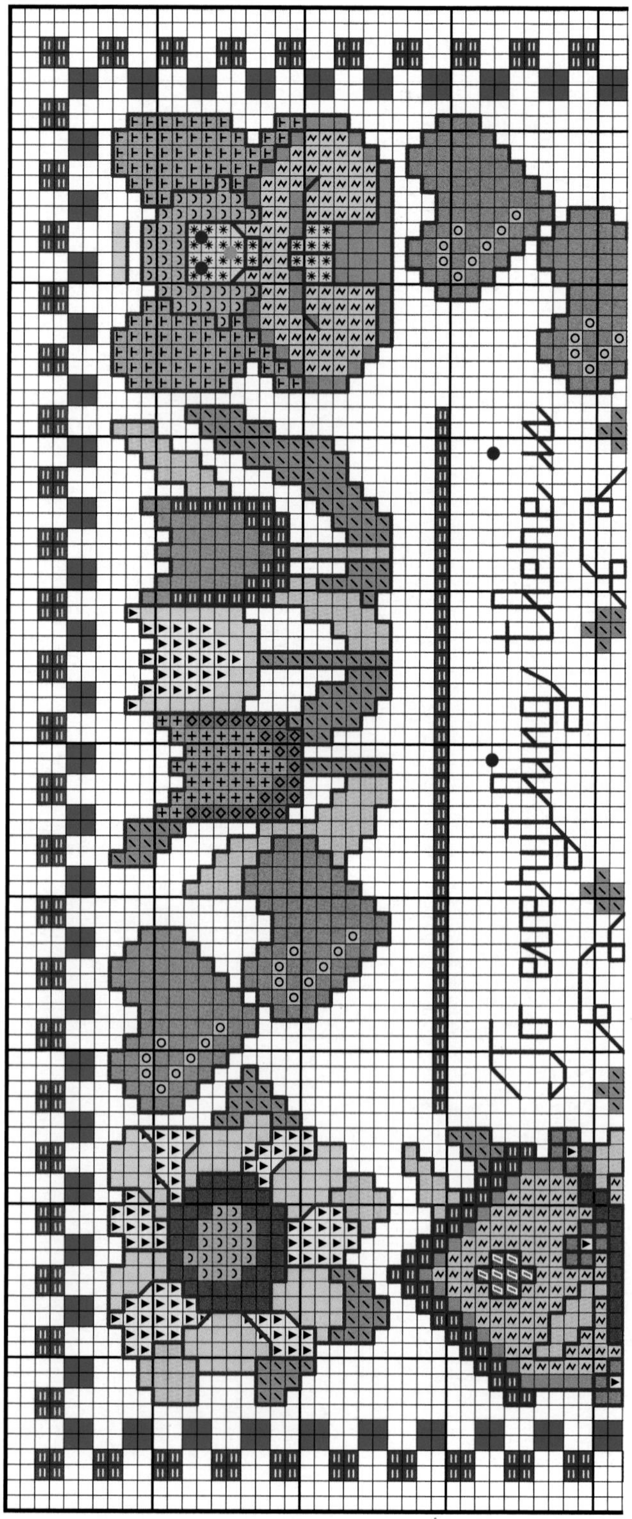

Chapter Five

As a chill wind blows, the verdant
landscape of Summer cloaks itself in
honeyed hues of gold and brown
foretelling the return of Winter's sleep.

Country
Autumn

Greet the changing seasons with lighthearted gladness,
stitching a burnished rainbow of floss
into cheerful portrayals of Autumn's bounty.

Trick or Treat

Designed by Christine A. Hendricks

Materials

- One 12" x 12" piece of willow green, one 11" x 12" piece of white and one 11" x 14" piece of white 14-count Aida
- ½ yd. fabric (for "Baa")
- ½ yd. fabric (for "Moo")
- Basket of choice
- Mounting board
- 1 yd. piping
- Bow of choice
- Craft glue or glue gun

Instructions

1: Center and stitch "Baa" design onto 12" x 12" piece of willow green Aida; "Moo" design onto 11" x 12" piece of white Aida; and "Hall-moo-ween" design onto 11" x 14" piece of white Aida, using two strands floss for Cross-Stitch and one strand floss for Backstitch and French Knot.

Notes: For "Baa" tote, trim design to 7½" x 8" for front. From fabric, cut one 7½" x 8" piece for back, two 3" x 8" pieces for sides, one 3" x 7½" piece for bottom and two 3" x 10" pieces for handles. For "Moo" tote, trim design to 7" x 7½" for front. From fabric, cut one 7" x 7½" piece for back, two 3" x 7½" pieces for sides, one 3" x 7" piece for bottom and two 3" x 10" pieces for handles. Use ½" seam allowance.

2: For each Tote, with right sides facing, sew front, back, sides and bottom together. Press under ½" on top edges of tote, sew in place.

3: For handles, with right sides facing, fold each piece in half lengthwise, sew long edges together. Turn right sides out; press. Position and sew one handle to front and one handle to back at top insides edges of tote as shown in photo.

Note: From mounting board, cut one 5⅜" x 7½" piece.

4: Center and mount "Hall-moo-ween" design over board. Glue piping to back outside edges of mounted design. Glue bow to top of mounted design as shown. Position and glue mounted design to front of basket as shown.

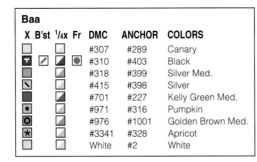

Baa

X	B'st	¼x	Fr	DMC	ANCHOR	COLORS
				#307	#289	Canary
			●	#310	#403	Black
				#318	#399	Silver Med.
				#415	#398	Silver
				#701	#227	Kelly Green Med.
				#971	#316	Pumpkin
				#976	#1001	Golden Brown Med.
				#3341	#328	Apricot
				White	#2	White

Baa
Stitch Count:
77 wide x 81 high

**Approximate
Design Size:**
11-count 7" x 7⅜"
14-count 5½" x 5⅞"
16-count 4⅞" x 5⅛"
18-count 4⅜" x 4½"
22-count 3½" x 3¾"

Baa

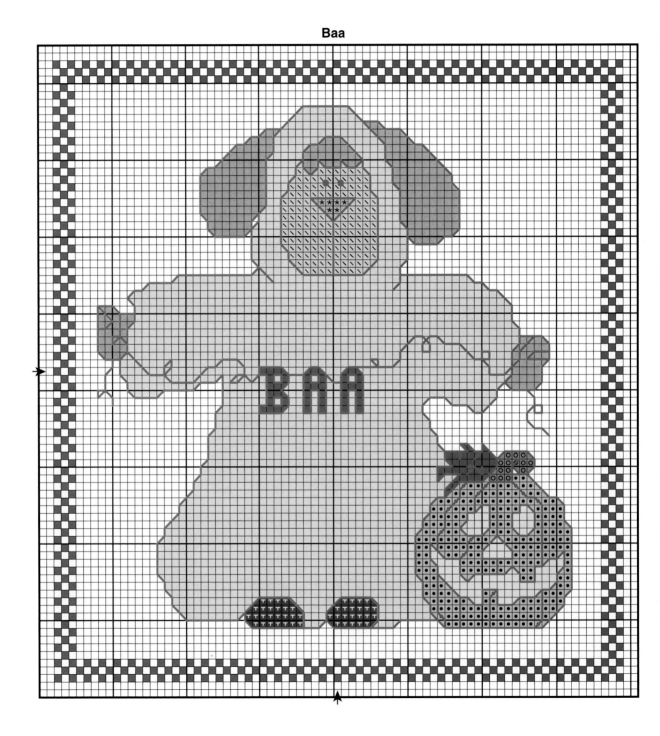

Hall-moo-ween

X	B'st	¼x	¾x	DMC	ANCHOR	COLORS		X	¼x	DMC	ANCHOR	COLORS
T	/			#310	#403	Black				#948	#1011	Peach Flesh Very Lt.
⊿			●	#353	#8	Peach Flesh Med.				#3799	#236	Charcoal Dk.
△				#413	#401	Charcoal				#3801	#35	Geranium Med.
				#553	#98	Violet Med.				White	#2	White
○				#666	#46	Geranium Dk.						

Hall-moo-ween

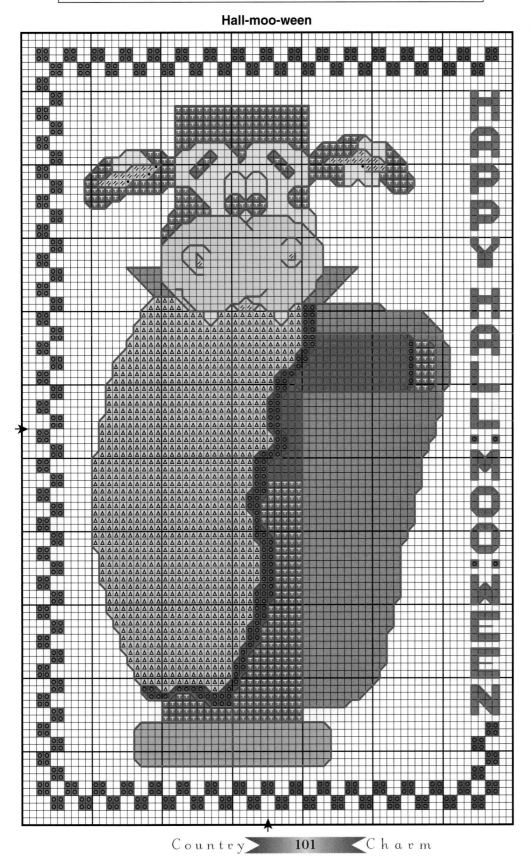

Hall-moo-ween Stitch Count:
66 wide x 104 high

Approximate Design Size:
11-count 6" x 9½"
14-count 4¾" x 7½"
16-count 4⅛" x 6½"
18-count 3¾" x 5⅞"
22-count 3" x 4¾"

Moo

X	B'st	¼x	Fr	DMC	ANCHOR	COLORS
★	✓	◣	●	#310	#403	Black
0		◣		#318	#399	Silver Med.
✓		◣		#353	#8	Peach Flesh Med.
▓		◣		#413	#401	Charcoal
✚		◣		#920	#1004	Copper Med.
▓	✓	◣		#947	#330	Burnt Orange
▒		◣		#951	#1010	Blush Lt.
☐		☐		White	#2	White

Moo
Stitch Count:
69 wide x 77 high

Approximate
Design Size:
11-count 6⅜" x 7"
14-count 5" x 5½"
16-count 4⅜" x 4⅞"
18-count 3⅞" x 4⅜"
22-count 3⅛" x 3½"

Moo

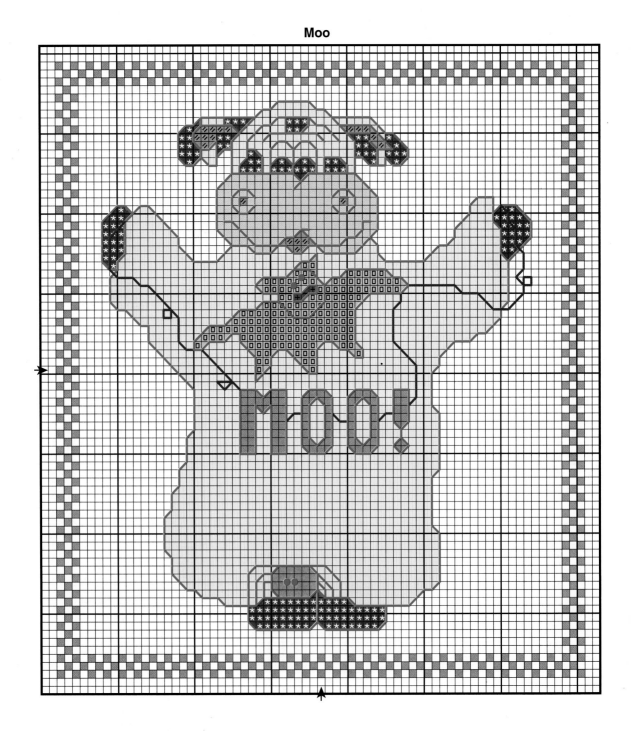

Pumpkin
Patch

Pumpkin Patch

Designed by Felicia L. Williams

Materials

• 14" x 16" piece of antique white 14-count Aida

Instructions

Center and stitch design, using two strands floss for Cross-Stitch and one strand floss for Backstitch and French Knot.

Stitch Count:
136 wide x 108 high

Approximate Design Size:
11-count 12⅜" x 9⅞"
14-count 9¾" x 7¾"
16-count 8½" x 6¾"
18-count 7⅝" x 6"
22-count 6¼" x 5"

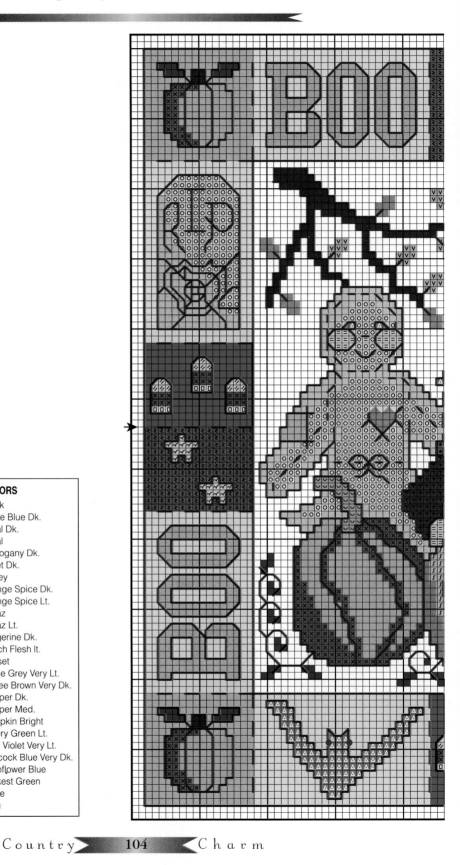

X	B'st	¼x	Fr	DMC	ANCHOR	COLORS
△	✎	◩	●	#310	#403	Black
	✎			#312	#979	Azure Blue Dk.
		◩		#349	#13	Coral Dk.
V				#351	#10	Coral
∪				#400	#351	Mahogany Dk.
≷				#552	#99	Violet Dk.
		◩		#676	#891	Honey
✕			●	#720	#326	Orange Spice Dk.
		◩		#722	#323	Orange Spice Lt.
☑				#726	#295	Topaz
0		◩		#727	#293	Topaz Lt.
S				#741	#304	Tangerine Dk.
≡		◩		#754	#1012	Peach Flesh lt.
+		◩		#782	#308	Russet
		◩		#822	#390	Beige Grey Very Lt.
				#898	#360	Coffee Brown Very Dk.
N				#918	#340	Copper Dk.
◉				#920	#1004	Copper Med.
				#970	#316	Pumpkin Bright
				#3364	#260	Celery Green Lt.
✳		◩		#3747	#120	Blue Violet Very Lt.
		◩		#3765	#170	Peacock Blue Very Dk.
▼		◩		#3807	#118	Cornflower Blue
				#3818	#212	Darkest Green
O		◩		White	#2	White
⁄		◩		Ecru	#387	Ecru

Lighten the atmosphere while reminding everyone to count their blessings by inviting these comical caricatures and their good-hearted humor to share the celebration.

Turkey Whimsies

Designed by Christine A. Hendricks

Materials

- One 11" x 12" piece and one 11" x 13" piece of white 14-count Aida
- Basket of choice
- Mounting board
- 1 yd. piping
- 1 yd. gathered ruffle
- Craft glue or glue gun

Instructions

1: Center and stitch "Give Thanks" design onto 11" x 12" piece and "Eat More Corn" design onto 11" x 13" piece of Aida, using two strands floss for Cross-Stitch and one strand floss for Backstitch and French Knot.

Note: From mounting board, cut one 5⅝" x 8" piece.

2: Center and mount "Eat More Corn" design over board. Glue piping, then ruffle to back outside edges of

Give Thanks
Stitch Count:
89 wide x 73 high

Approximate Design Size:
11-count 8⅛" x 6⅝"
14-count 6⅜" x 5¼"
16-count 5⅝" x 4⅝"
18-count 5" x 4⅛"
22-count 4⅛" x 3⅜"

Give Thanks

X	¼x	DMC	ANCHOR	COLORS	X	B'st	¼x	Fr	DMC	ANCHOR	COLORS
★		#666	#46	Geranium Dk.					#951	#1010	Blush Lt.
		#740	#316	Pumpkin Bright					#958	#187	Aquamarine Med.
◎		#920	#1004	Copper Med.					#977	#1002	Golden Brown
◢		#922	#1003	Copper Lt.		✓		●	#3371	#382	Darkest Brown

Give Thanks

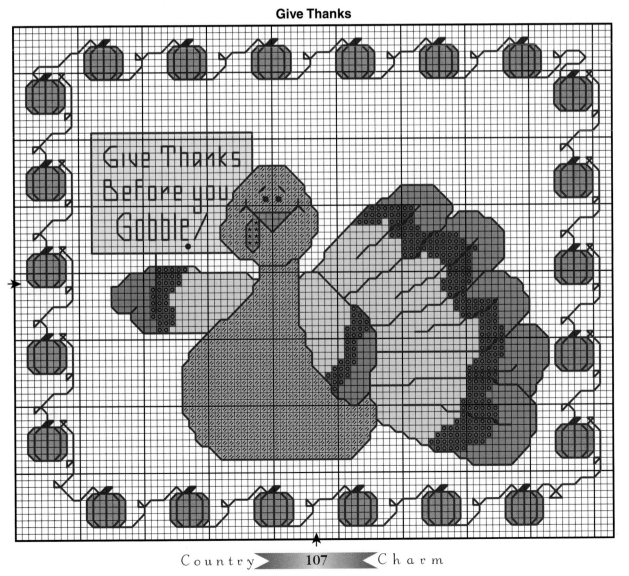

mounted design. Position and
glue mounted design to front of
basket as shown in photo.

Eat More Corn
Stitch Count:
99 wide x 67 high

**Approximate
Design Size:**
11-count 9" x 6⅛"
14-count 7⅛" x 4⅞"
16-count 6¼" x 4¼"
18-count 5½" x 3¾"
22-count 4½" x 3⅛"

Eat More Corn

X	¼x				ANCHOR	COLORS	X	B'st	Fr	¼x		DMC	ANCHOR	COLORS
				#224	#893	Victorian Rose Lt.					#741	#304	Tangerine Dk.
				#225	#1026	Victorian Rose Pale					#958	#187	Aquamarine Med.
				#307	#289	Canary					#976	#1001	Golden Brown Med.
				#666	#46	Geranium Dk.					#3371	#382	Darkest Brown

Eat More Corn

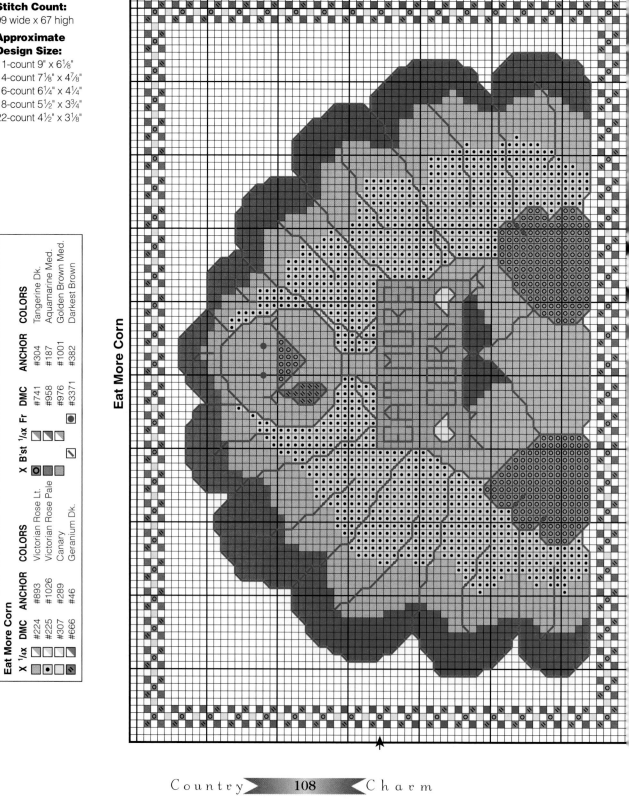

Halloween

Halloween

Designed by Mike Vickery

Materials
- 11" x 18" piece of mushroom 14-count Linaida

Instructions
Center and stitch design, using two strands floss for Cross-Stitch and one strand floss for Backstitch.

Stitch Count:
166 wide x 74 high

Approximate Design Size:
11-count 15⅛" x 6¾"
14-count 11⅞" x 5⅜"
16-count 10⅜" x 4⅝"
18-count 9¼" x 4⅛"
22-count 7⅝" x 3⅜"

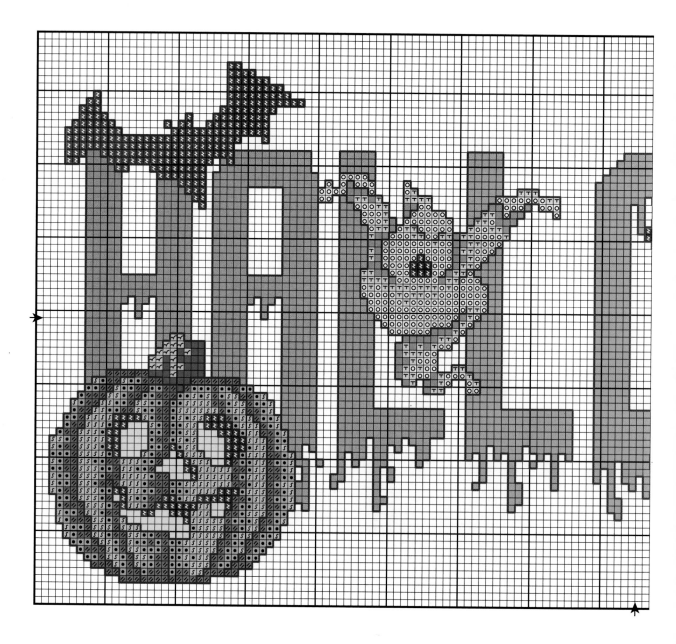

X	DMC	ANCHOR	COLORS	X B'st	DMC	ANCHOR	COLORS
	#307	#289	Canary	0	#762	#234	Silver Very Lt.
⊠	#310	#403	Black	⊤	#775	#128	Baby Blue
	#318	#399	Silver Med.		#971	#316	Pumpkin
↰	#434	#310	Darkest Toast	⊠	#3021	#905	Brown Grey
△	#436	#1045	Toast	◺	#3325	#129	Delft Blue
	#470	#267	Avocado Green Lt.		#3778	#1013	Terra Cotta
✔	#472	#253	Avocado Green Pale	◿	#3799	#236	Charcoal Dk.
✳	#720	#326	Orange Spice Dk.	∫	#3825	#323	Orange Spice Very Lt.
⁄	#721	#324	Orange Spice Med.	0	White	#2	White
•	#722	#323	Orange Spice Lt.				

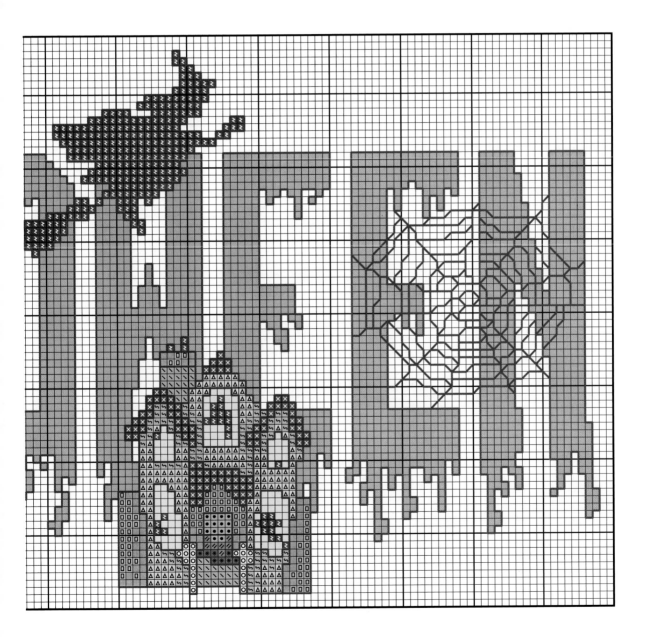

Bushels of love flow from this appealing birth sampler deliciously stitched with charming flair and personalized especially for your little sweetie pie.

Apple of My Eye

Designed by Thomas C. Williams

Materials

• 11" x 13" piece of white
  14-count Aida

Instructions

Select desired letters
and numbers for name
and date from Alphabet &
Numbers graph, center
and stitch design, using
two strands floss for
Cross-Stitch and one
strand floss for Backstitch
and French Knot.

Stitch Count:
69 wide x 92 high

**Approximate
Design Size:**
11-count 6⅜" x 8⅜"
14-count 5" x 6⅝"
16-count 4⅜" x 5¾"
18-count 3⅞" x 5⅛"
22-count 3⅛" x 4¼"

Alphabet & Numbers

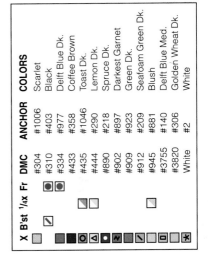

X	B'st	¼x	Fr	DMC	ANCHOR	COLORS
				#304	#1006	Scarlet
				#310	#403	Black
				#334	#977	Delft Blue Dk.
				#433	#358	Coffee Brown
				#435	#1046	Toast Dk.
				#444	#290	Lemon Dk.
				#890	#218	Spruce Dk.
				#902	#897	Darkest Garnet
				#909	#923	Green Dk.
				#912	#209	Seafoam Green Dk.
				#945	#881	Blush
				#3755	#140	Delft Blue Med.
				#3820	#306	Golden Wheat Dk.
				White	#2	White

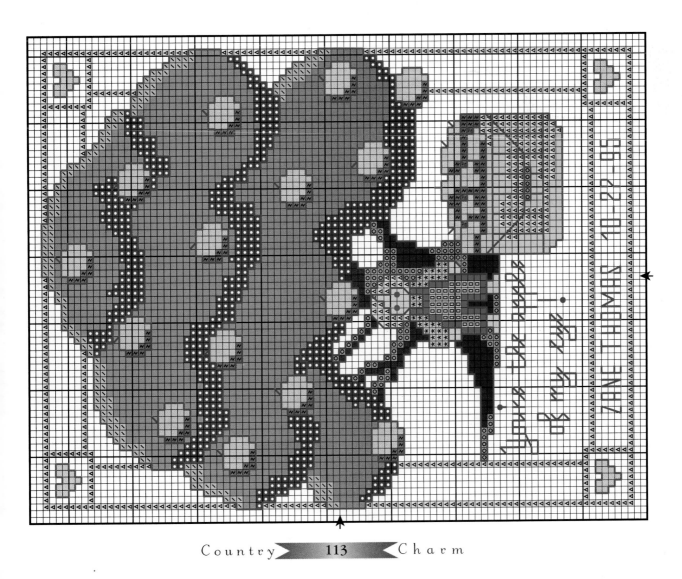

Country Ladies

Designed by Felicia L. Williams

Materials
- 12" x 15" piece of Confederate grey 14-count Aida
- Bread box of choice
- Mounting board
- 1 yd. rickrack
- Craft glue or glue gun

Instructions

1: Center and stitch design, using two strands floss for Cross-Stitch and one strand floss for Backstitch and French Knot.

   Note: From mounting board, cut one 6½" x 9½" piece.

   2: Center and mount design over board. Glue rickrack to back outside edges of mounted design. Position and glue mounted design to bread box as shown in photo.

Country flavor at its best is yours morning, noon and night when you let this wholesome trio spread a little sunshine with their fresh-from-the-farm charm.

**Approximate
Design Size:**
11-count 11³⁄₈" x 7⁵⁄₈"
14-count 8⁷⁄₈" x 6"
16-count 7³⁄₄" x 5¹⁄₄"
18-count 7" x 4⁵⁄₈"
22-count 5⁵⁄₈" x 3⁷⁄₈"

X	B'st	¹⁄₄x	Fr	DMC	ANCHOR	COLORS
△				#225	#1026	Victorian Rose Pale
⧖		◩		#304	#1006	Scarlet
⧄		◩	●	#309	#42	Rose Deep
⋈	◩	◩	●	#310	#403	Black
▢		◩		#335	#38	Rose Pink Dk.
●				#353	#8	Peach Flesh Med.
✚				#367	#217	Pistachio Green Dk.
▦		◩		#368	#214	Pistachio Green Lt.
◱				#369	#1043	Pistachio Green Pale
⑀				#372	#853	Camel Lt.
⊟				#435	#1046	Toast Dk.
▢		◻		#676	#891	Honey
ⅅ				#677	#886	Honey Lt.
◯		◩		#762	#234	Silver Very Lt.
◡				#792	#941	Cornflower Blue Dk.
▨				#793	#176	Cornflower Blue Lt.
★				#794	#175	Cornflower Blue Very Lt.
⊤				#869	#944	Warm Brown Med.
⊠		◩		#946	#332	Burnt Orange Dk.
▢		◻		#951	#1010	Blush Lt.
▽				#970	#316	Pumpkin Bright
▨				#976	#1001	Golden Brown Med.
⋁		◻		#977	#1002	Golden Brown
▽				#3756	#1037	Baby Blue Very Lt.
◣				#3770	#1009	Cream Lt.
②				#3823	#275	Topaz Very Pale
▢		◻		White	#2	White

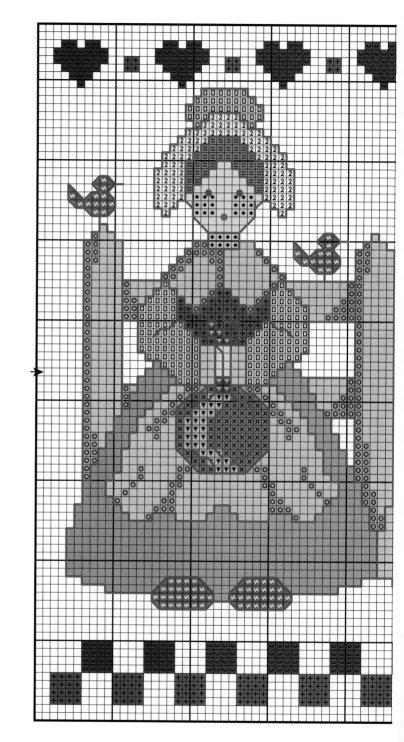

Harvest Welcome

Designed by Felicia L. Williams

Materials

- 14" x 16" piece of white 14-count Aida

Instructions

Center and stitch design, using two strands floss for Cross-Stitch and one strand floss for Backstitch and French Knot.

Handpicked just for you, this dandy rural duo will let you reap the benefits of sunny smiles galore when they greet friends and loved-ones at your next gathering.

Stitch Count:
136 wide x 107 high

Approximate Design Size:
11-count 12⅜" x 9¾"
14-count 9¾" x 7¾"
16-count 8½" x 6¾"
18-count 7⅝" x 6"
22-count 6¼" x 4⅞"

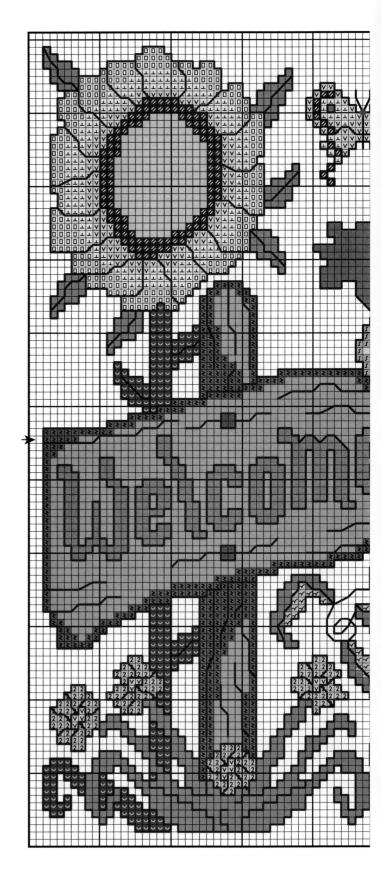

X	B'st	¼x	³/4x	Fr	DMC	ANCHOR	COLORS
■	▧	◪		◉	#310	#403	Black
S					#353	#8	Peach Flesh Med.
T					#402	#1047	Copper Very Lt.
®		◪			#611	#898	Butternut Dk.
					#738	#361	Toast Very Lt.
◤					#762	#234	Silver Very Lt.
					#783	#307	Topaz Very Dk.
◡					#890	#218	Spruce Dk.
					#904	#258	Darkest Parrot Green
☑					#907	#255	Parrot Green Lt.
■					#921	#1004	Copper
✚		◪			#922	#1003	Copper Lt.
◿					#938	#381	Darkest Mahogany
D					#946	#332	Burnt Orange Dk.
☐		☐			#951	#1010	Blush Lt.
2					#961	#76	Antique Rose Dk.
O					#970	#316	Pumpkin Bright
⊥		☐			#973	#297	Lemon
★					#3033	#391	Beige Grey Pale
0					#3078	#292	Yellow Cream
■		◪			#3705	#35	Carnation Dk.
▼		☐			#3755	#140	Delft Blue Med.
					#3760	#161	Peacock Blue Dk.
V		☐	⊡		#3820	#306	Golden Wheat Dk.
●		☐			White	#2	White

Chapter Six

Energize your surroundings with
uplifting scenes and thoughtful sayings
that will guide your way
to the silver lining in any cloud.

Country
Inspirations

Provoke your heart to good deeds and rejuvenate your spirit
with encouraging words that lend new meaning
to the ageless adage of "a stitch in time."

Every house where love abides
And friendship is a guest
Is surely home sweet home
For there the heart can rest

Where Love Abides

Designed by Carla Acosta

Materials

- 11" x 15" piece of light oatmeal 14-count Fiddler's Lite®
- ⅔ yd. fabric
- ⅛ yd. coordinating fabric
- Batting
- Black thread

Instructions

1: Center and stitch design, using two strands floss for Cross-Stitch and one strand floss for Backstitch.

Notes: Trim design to 7" x 10". From fabric, cut two 4" x 10" for A pieces, two 4" x 14" for B pieces and one 14" x 17" piece for back. From coordinating fabric, cut thirty-two 1¼" x 1¼" pieces for squares. From batting, cut one 14" x 17" piece. Use ¼" seam allowance.

2: With right sides facing, sew design, A and B pieces together according to Front Assembly Diagram, forming front. With wrong sides facing and batting between, pin front and back together. Using black thread and running stitch, and sewing through all thicknesses, sew front and back together along outside edges as shown in photo, forming wall hanging. Using black thread and running stitch, and sewing through all thicknesses, sew squares to wall hanging according to Square Placement Diagram.

Front Assembly Diagram

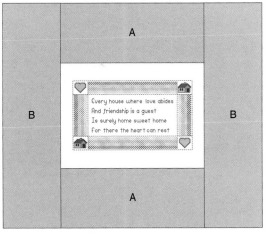

Square Placement Diagram

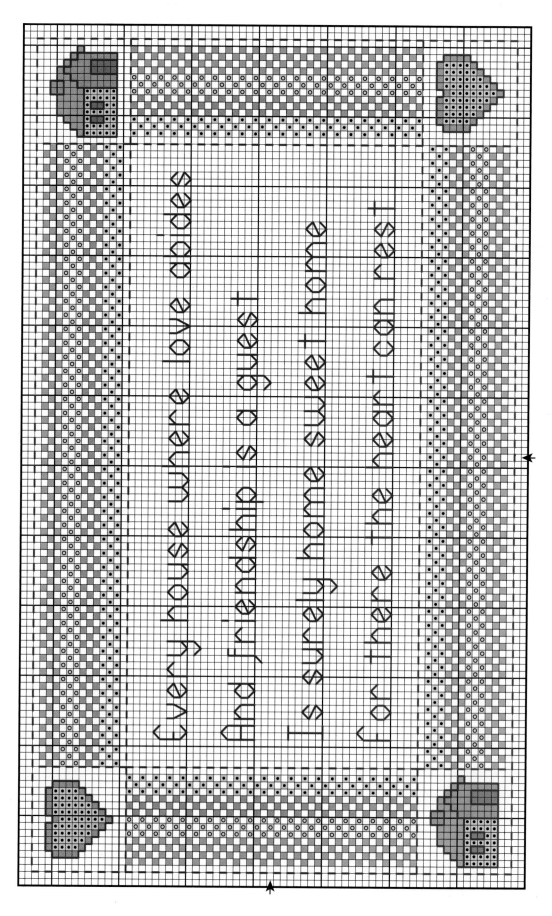

Stitch Count:
119 wide x 71 high

Approximate Design Size:
11-count 10⅞" x 6½"
14-count 8½" x 5⅛"
16-count 7½" x 4½"
18-count 6⅝" x 4"
22-count 5½" x 3¼"

X	B'st	DMC	ANCHOR	COLORS
▨		#930	#1035	Blue Denim Dk.
▨		#931	#1034	Blue Denim Med.
▨	◿	#3371	#382	Darkest Brown
▨		#3726	#1018	Antique Mauve Dk.
•		#3727	#1016	Antique Mauve

Every house where love abides

And friendship is a guest

Is surely home sweet home

For there the heart can rest

I Count
You Twice

I Count You Twice

Designed by Carla Acosta

Materials

- 12" x 16" piece of ivory 16-count Aida

Instructions

Select desired letters and numbers for initials and year from Alphabet & Numbers graph, center and stitch design, using two strands floss for Cross-Stitch and one strand floss for Backstitch.

Stitch Count:
97 wide x 158 high

Approximate Design Size:
11-count 8⅞" x 14⅜"
14-count 7" x 11⅜"
16-count 6⅛" x 9⅞"
18-count 5⅜" x 8⅞"
22-count 4½" x 7¼"

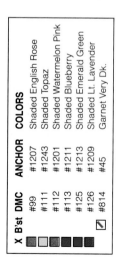

X	B'st	DMC	ANCHOR	COLORS
		#99	#1207	Shaded English Rose
		#111	#1243	Shaded Topaz
		#112	#1201	Shaded Watermelon Pink
		#113	#1211	Shaded Blueberry
		#125	#1213	Shaded Emerald Green
		#126	#1209	Shaded Lt. Lavender
		#814	#45	Garnet Very Dk.

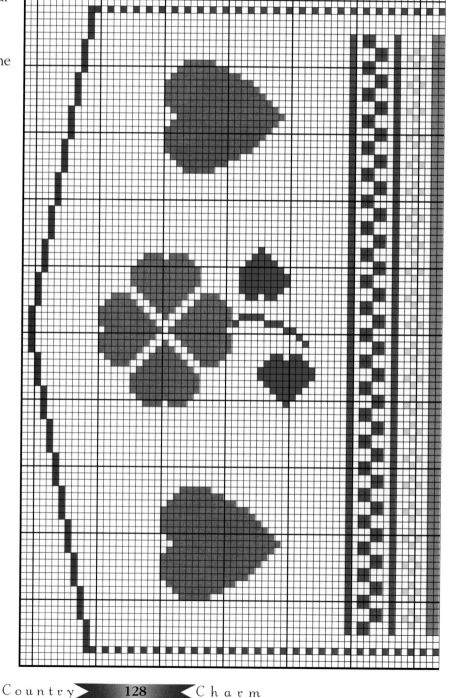

Alphabet & Numbers

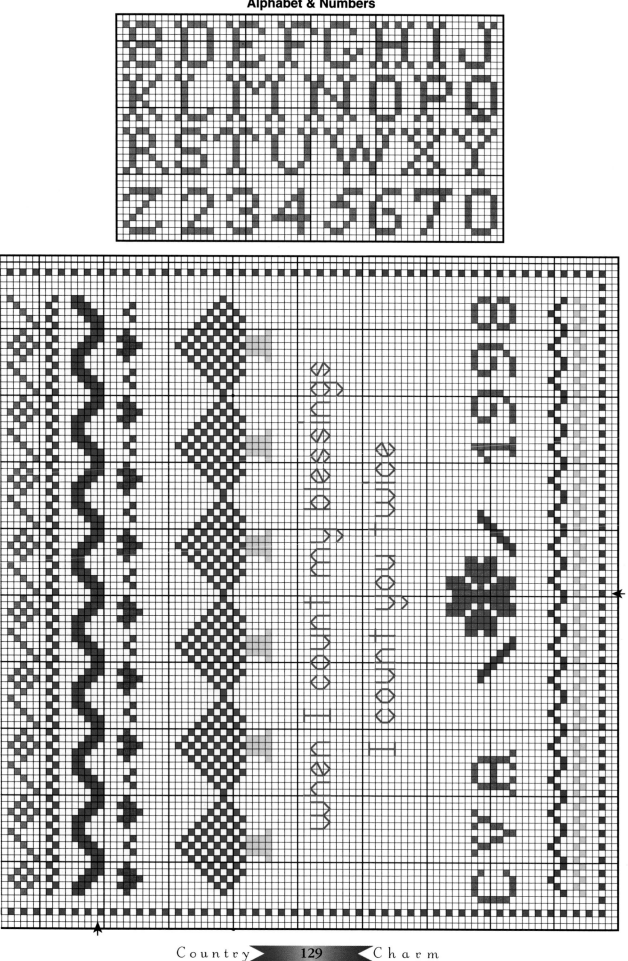

a soft answer turneth away wrath PRO. 15:1

Gentle words of wisdom surrounded by an artistic patchwork frame will inspire you to rejuvenate your mind through the thoughtful tranquility of daily meditation.

A Soft Answer

Designed by Sherry Parker Hughes

Materials
- 12" x 13" piece of white 14-count Aida
- ⅓ yd. fabric #1
- ¼ yd. fabric #2
- ⅓ yd. fabric #3
- ¾ yd. fabric #4
- 16" x 16" pillow form

Instructions

1: Center and stitch design, using two strands floss for Cross-Stitch and one strand floss for Backstitch and French Knot.

Notes: Trim design to 9½" x 9½". From fabric #1, cut two 1¾" x 11" for A pieces, two 1¾" x 9½" for B pieces and 10 pieces according to Triangle Pattern. From fabric #2, cut 10 pieces according to Triangle Pattern. From fabric #3, cut two 1¾" x 16" for E pieces, two 1¾" x 17½" for F pieces and 10 pieces according to Triangle Pattern. From fabric #4, cut two 12" x 17½" pieces for back and 10 pieces according to Triangle Pattern. Use ½" seam allowance.

2: For C pieces, with right sides facing, sew fabric #1 and fabric #4 triangles together, forming ten 3½"-square blocks; for D pieces, repeat with fabric #2 and fabric #3 triangles, forming ten 3½"-square blocks.

3: For front, with right sides facing, sew design, A, B, C, D, E and F pieces together according to Front Assembly Diagram.

4: Hem one 17½" edge of each back piece. Place one hemmed edge over the other, overlapping enough to create a 17½" x 17½" back with opening. Baste outside edges together; press.

5: With right sides facing, sew front and back together. Trim seam and turn right sides out; press. Insert pillow form.

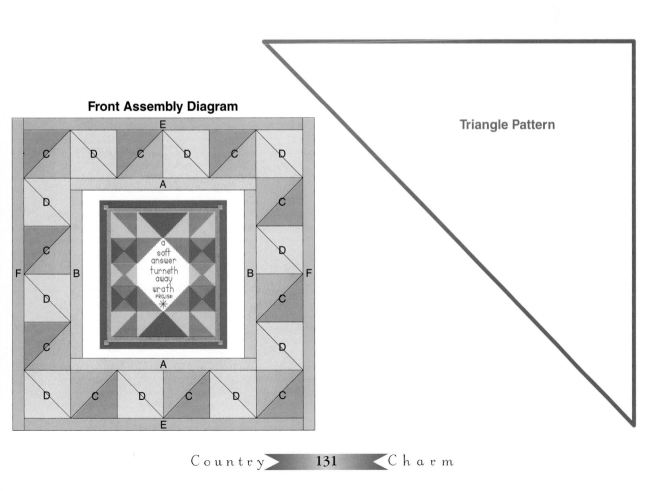

Front Assembly Diagram

Triangle Pattern

Stitch Count:
88 wide x 99 high

**Approximate
Design Size:**
11-count 8" x 9"
14-count 6⅜" x 7⅛"
16-count 5½" x 6¼"
18-count 5" x 5½"
22-count 4" x 4½"

X	B'st	Fr	DMC	ANCHOR	COLORS
⬜			#415	#398	Silver
⬛	✎	◉	#823	#152	Navy Blue Very Dk.
⬛			#902	#897	Darkest Garnet
⬜			#931	#1034	Blue Denim Med.
⬜			#3688	#66	Mauve

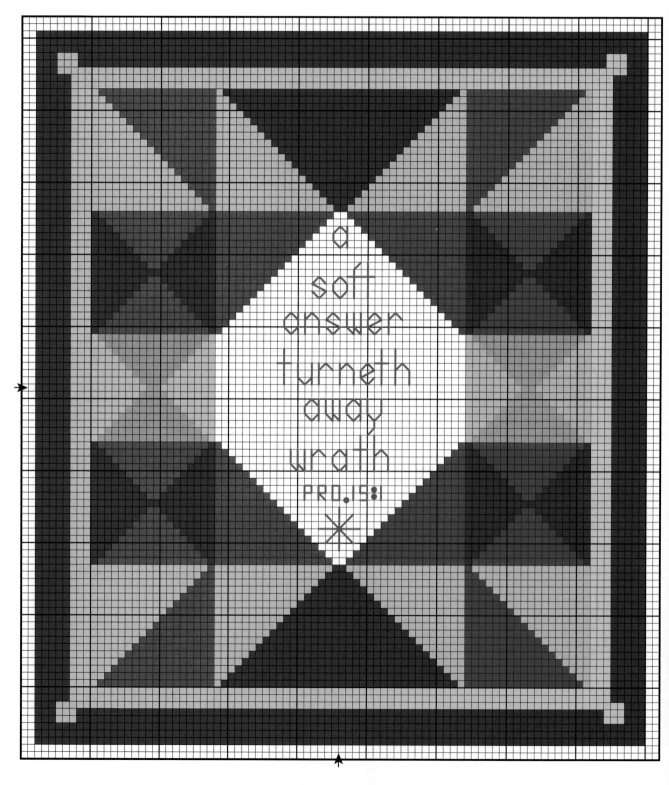

Joy, Patience & Faith

Joy, Patience & Faith

Designed by Felicia L. Williams

Materials

- 13" x 15" piece of misty blue 14-count Aida

Instructions

Center and stitch design, using two strands floss for Cross-Stitch and one strand floss for Backstitch and French Knot.

Stitch Count:

95 wide x 130 high

Approximate Design Size:

11-count 8⅝" x 11⅞"
14-count 6⅞" x 9⅜"
16-count 6" x 8⅛"
18-count 5⅜" x 7¼"
22-count 4⅜" x 6"

X	B'st	¼x	Fr	DMC	ANCHOR	COLORS
				#309	#42	Rose Deep
				#310	#403	Black
				#312	#979	Azure Blue Dk.
				#334	#977	Delft Blue Dk.
				#712	#926	Cream Very Pale
				#725	#305	Topaz Med.
				#745	#300	Topaz Very Lt.
				#3041	#871	Antique Violet
				#3042	#870	Antique Violet Lt.
				#3325	#129	Delft Blue
				#3713	#1020	Salmon Very Lt.
				#3726	#1018	Antique Mauve Dk.
				#3733	#75	Dusty Rose Lt.
				#3743	#869	Antique Violet Very Lt.
				#3752	#1032	Blue Denim Very Lt.
				#3774	#778	Fawn Lt.
				#3779	#868	Terra Cotta Very Lt.
				#3815	#216	Celdon Green Dk.
				#3817	#213	Celdon Green Lt.
				#3822	#295	Golden Wheat Lt.
				#3828	#888	Hazel Nut

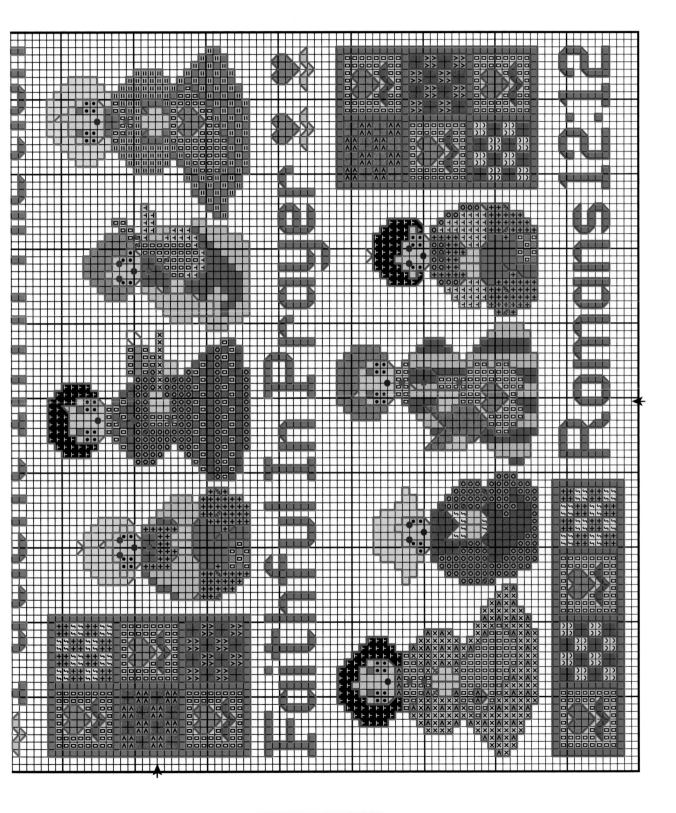

Embrace the changing seasons with this not-quite-so-perfect heavenly mis... to brighten up your home with her demure face and patchwork wings.

Autumn Angel

Designed by Felicia L. Williams

Materials

- 10" x 11" piece of white 14-count Aida
- Ceramic button of choice
- Basket of choice
- Mounting board
- ⅔ yd. rickrack
- Desired amount of ribbon
- Craft glue or glue gun

Instructions

1: Center and stitch design, using two strands floss for Cross-Stitch and one strand floss for Backstitch and French Knot. Use one strand coordinating floss for securing beads. Secure ceramic button to design as shown in photo.

Note: From mounting board, cut one 3⅞" x 5⅜" piece.

2: Center and mount design over board. Glue rickrack to back outside edges of design. Position and glue mounted design to basket as shown. Decorate basket with ribbon as shown or as desired.

Stitch Count:
50 wide x 70 high

Approximate Design Size:
11-count 4⅝" x 6⅜"
14-count 3⅝" x 5"
16-count 3⅛" x 4⅜"
18-count 2⅞" x 4"
22-count 2⅜" x 3¼"

X	B'st	¼x	Fr	DMC	ANCHOR	COLORS
		▨		#300	#352	Mahogany Very Dk.
	▨	▨	●	#310	#403	Black
▨				#320	#215	Pistachio Green Med.
▽				#356	#5975	Terra Cotta Med.
T				#368	#214	Pistachio Green Lt.
		▨		#369	#1043	Pistachio Green Pale
+				#402	#1047	Copper Very Lt.
✕				#822	#390	Beige Grey Very Lt.
				#932	#1033	Blue Denim Lt.
☐		▨		#945	#881	Blush
				#962	#75	Antique Rose Med.
	▨			#972	#298	Tangerine Med.
	▨			#986	#246	Pistachio Green Ultra Dk.
☐				#3078	#292	Yellow Cream
☐		▨		#3820	#306	Golden Wheat Dk.
V				#3822	#295	Golden Wheat Lt.
●				#3824	#8	Apricot Lt.
▤			●	#3830	#341	Terra Cotta Dk.
▷				White	#2	White

SEED BEADS

⊡	#00479	White			

Quilt Sampler

Designed by Thomas C. & Felicia L. Williams

Materials
- 14" x 18" piece of antique white 14-count Aida

Stitch Count:
116 wide x 164 high

Approximate Design Size:
11-count 10⅝" x 15"
14-count 8⅜" x 11¾"
16-count 7¼" x 10¼"
18-count 6½" x 9⅛"
22-count 5⅜" x 7½"

Instructions
Select desired letters and numbers for name and date, center and stitch design, using two strands floss for Cross-Stitch and one strand floss for Backstitch and French Knot.

Celebrate the joyous union of husband and wife as they begin their journey, collecting memories one by one to form the fabric of their life.

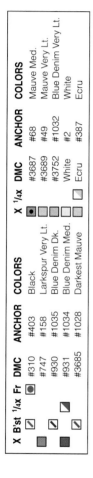

X	B'st	1/4x	Fr	DMC	ANCHOR	COLORS
			◉	#310	#403	Black
				#747	#158	Larkspur Very Lt.
				#930	#1035	Blue Denim Dk.
				#931	#1034	Blue Denim Med.
				#3685	#1028	Darkest Mauve

X	1/4x	DMC	ANCHOR	COLORS
●		#3687	#68	Mauve Med.
		#3689	#49	Mauve Very Lt.
		#3752	#1032	Blue Denim Very Lt.
		White	#2	White
		Ecru	#387	Ecru

GOD REST THIS LOVE

UPON THIS DOOR

AND

BLESS THIS HOUSE

FOREVERMORE

Noah's Ark

Noah's Ark

Designed by Louise Young

Materials

- One 12" x 14" piece and one 12" x 16" piece of natural brown 10-count Betsy Ross Linen
- One crow (right facing), one large star and two dove buttons

Instructions

Center and stitch "Noah's Boat" design onto 12" x 14" piece and "Noah's Walk" design onto 12" x 16" piece of Betsy Ross Linen, using four strands floss for Cross-Stitch and two strands floss for Backstitch. Use 12 strands coordinating floss to secure one dove, crow and star buttons to "Noah's Boat" design and remaining dove button to "Noah's Walk" design as shown in photo.

**Noah's Boat
Stitch Count:**
81 wide x 57 high

**Approximate
Design Size:**
10-count 8⅛" x 5¾"
11-count 7⅜" x 5¼"
14-count 5⅞" x 4⅛"
16-count 5⅛" x 3⅝"
18-count 4½" x 3¼"
22-count 3¾" x 2⅝"

Noah's Boat

X	DMC	ANCHOR	COLORS	X B'st	DMC	ANCHOR	COLORS
	#208	#110	Lavender Dk.		#799	#136	Blueberry Med.
	#310	#403	Black		#816	#20	Garnet Med.
	#319	#218	Spruce		#922	#1003	Copper Lt.
	#336	#150	Indigo Blue		#3781	#1050	Coffee Brown
	#356	#5975	Terra Cotta Med.		#3821	#305	Golden Wheat
	#738	#361	Toast Very Lt.		White	#2	White

Noah's Walk

Noah's Walk Stitch Count:
61 wide x 97 high

Approximate Design Size:
10-count 6⅛" x 9¾"
11-count 5⅝" x 8⅞"
14-count 4⅜" x 7"
16-count 3⅞" x 6⅛"
18-count 3⅜" x 5⅜"
22-count 2⅞" x 4½"

Goals Are Like Stars

Designed by Jacquelyn Fox

Materials
- 11" x 12" piece of Victorian blue 14-count Yorkshire Aida

Instructions
Center and stitch design, using two strands floss for Cross-Stitch, Backstitch and French Knot of lettering. Use one strand floss for remaining Backstitch and French Knot.

Spur those you love to seek stellar results, no matter what the feat, with a comfortable childhood friend to help them find their way.

X	B'st	1/4x	Fr	DMC	ANCHOR	COLORS
■				#319	#218	Spruce
+				#320	#215	Pistachio Green Med.
	/	◢	◉	#413	#401	Charcoal
▨				#422	#373	Hazel Nut Lt.
▨				#502	#877	Sage Green Med.
⋈	/	◢		#727	#293	Topaz Lt.
▨		◢		#869	#944	Warm Brown Med.
▨				#3078	#292	Yellow Cream
◎				#3768	#779	Sea Mist Dk.
⊡	/		◉	#3781	#1050	Coffee Brown
✕		◢		#3828	#888	Hazel Nut

Stitch Count:
84 wide x 64 high

Approximate Design Size:
11-count 7⅝" x 5⅞"
14-count 6" x 4⅝"
16-count 5¼" x 4"
18-count 4¾" x 3⅝"
22-count 3⅞" x 3"

General Instructions

Tools of the Stitcher

Perforated paper has holes evenly spaced for 14 stitches per inch.

Fabrics

Most counted cross-stitch projects are worked on evenweave fabrics made especially for counted thread embroidery. These fabrics have vertical and horizontal threads of uniform thickness and spacing. Aida cloth is a favorite of beginning stitchers because its weave forms distinctive squares in the fabric, which makes placing stitches easy. To determine a fabric's thread count, count the number of threads per inch of fabric.

Linen is made from fibers of the flax plant and is strong and durable. Its lasting quality makes it the perfect choice for heirloom projects. Linen is available in a range of muted colors and stitch counts.

In addition to evenweave fabrics, many stitchers enjoy using waste canvas and perforated paper. Waste canvas is basted to clothing or other fabric, forming a grid for stitching which is later removed.

Needles

Cross-stitch needles should have elongated eyes and blunt points. They should slip easily between the threads of the fabric, but should not pierce the fabric. The most common sizes used for cross-stitching are size 24 or 26. The ideal needle size is just small enough to slip easily through your fabric. Some stitchers prefer to use a slightly smaller needle for backstitching. When stitching on waste canvas, use a sharp needle.

Hoops, Frames & Scissors

Hoops can be round or oval and come in many sizes. The three main types are plastic, spring-tension and wooden. Frames are easier on the fabric than hoops and come in many sizes and shapes. Once fabric is mounted it doesn't have to be removed until stitching is complete, saving fabric from excessive handling.

Small, sharp scissors are essential for cutting floss and removing mistakes. For cutting fabrics, invest in a top-quality pair of medium-sized sewing scissors. To keep them in top form, use these scissors only for cutting fabrics and floss.

Stitching Threads

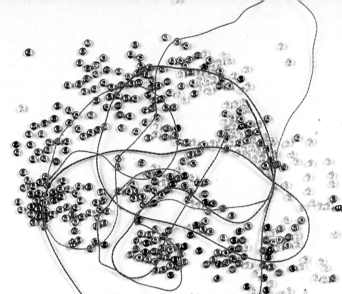

Today's cross-stitcher can achieve a vast array of effects in texture, color and shine. In addition to the perennial favorite, six-strand floss, stitchers can choose from sparkling metallics, shiny rayons, silks, narrow ribbon threads and much more.

Six-Strand Floss

Six-strand floss comes in a variety of colors and is available in metallics, silk and rayon as well as cotton. Most projects are worked using two or three strands of floss for cross-stitches and one or two strands for backstitches. For ease of stitching and to prevent wear on fibers, use lengths no longer than 18".

Pearl Cotton

Pearl cotton is available in #3, #5, #8 and #12, with #3 being the thickest. The plies of pearl cotton will not separate, and for most stitching one strand is used. Pearl cotton has a lustrous sheen.

Flower & Ribbon Threads

Flower thread has a tight twist and comes in many soft colors. It is heavier than one ply of six-strand floss – one strand of flower thread equals two strands of floss. Ribbon thread is a narrow ribbon especially created for stitching. It comes in a large number of colors in satin as well as metallic finishes.

Blending Filament & Metallic Braid

Blending filament is a fine, shiny fiber that can be used alone or combined with floss or other thread. Knotting the blending filament on the needle with a slipknot is recommended for control.

Metallic braid is a braided metallic fiber, usually used single-ply. Thread this fiber

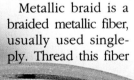

SLIPKNOT

just as you would any other fiber. Use short lengths, about 15", to keep the fiber from fraying.

Stitching with Beads

Small seed beads can be added to any cross-stitch design, using one bead per stitch. Knot thread at beginning of beaded section for security, especially if you are adding beads to clothing. The bead should lie in the same direction as the top half of cross-stitches.

Bead Attachment

Use one strand floss to secure beads. Bring beading needle up from back of work, leaving 2" length of thread hanging; do not knot (end will be secured between stitches as you work). Thread bead on needle; complete stitch.

Do not skip over more than two stitches or spaces without first securing thread, or last bead will be loose. To secure, weave thread into several stitches on back of work. Follow graph to work design, using one bead per stitch.

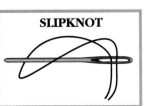

Before You Begin

Assemble fabric, floss, pattern and tools. Familiarize yourself with the graph, color key and instructions before beginning.

Preparing Fabric

Before you stitch, decide how large to cut fabric. If you are making a pillow or other design which requires a large unstitched area, be sure to leave plenty of fabric. If you are making a small project, leave at least 3" around all edges of design. Determine the design area size by using this formula: number of stitches across design area divided by the number of threads per inch of fabric equals size of fabric in inches. Measure fabric, then cut evenly along horizontal and vertical threads.

Press out folds. To prevent raveling, hand overcast or machine zigzag fabric edges. Find center of fabric by folding horizontally and vertically, and mark with a small stitch.

Reading Graphs

Cross-stitch graphs or charts are made up of colors and symbols to tell you the exact color, type and placement of each stitch. Each square represents the area for one complete cross-stitch. Next to each graph, there is a key with information about stitches and floss colors represented by the graph's colors and symbols.

Color keys have abbreviated headings for cross-stitch (x), one-half cross-stitch (½x), quarter cross-stitch (¼x), three-quarter cross-stitch (¾x), backstitch (B'st), French knot (Fr), lazy daisy stitch (LzD) and straight stitch (Str). Some graphs are so large they must be divided for printing.

Preparing Floss

The six strands of floss are easily separated, and the number of strands used is given in instructions. Cut strands in 14"-18" lengths. When separating floss, always separate all six strands, then recombine the number of strands needed. To make floss separating easier, run cut length across a damp sponge. To prevent floss from tangling, run cut length through a fabric-softener dryer sheet before separating and threading needle. To colorfast red floss tones, which sometimes bleed, hold floss under running water until water runs clear. Allow to air dry.

X	B'st	DMC	ANCHOR	COLORS
		#300	#352	Mahogany Very Dk.
		#301	#1049	Cinnamon Lt.
	✓	#310	#403	Black
		#498	#1005	Garnet
		#702	#226	Kelly Green Lt.
		#703	#238	Parrot Green
		#712	#926	Cream Very Pale
		#718	#88	Plum Med.
		#745	#300	Topaz Very Lt.
		#781	#309	Russet Med.
		#782	#308	Russet
		#783	#307	Topaz Very Dk.
	✓	#796	#133	Royal Blue
		#798	#131	Blueberry Dk.
		#814	#45	Garnet Very Dk.
		#822	#390	Beige Grey Very Lt.
		#828	#158	Larkspur Lt.
		#915	#1029	Plum Very Dk.
		#937	#268	Black Avocado
		#3325	#129	Delft Blue
		#3820	#306	Golden Wheat Dk.

Stitching Techniques

Beginning & Ending a Thread

Try these methods for beginning a thread, then decide which one is best for you.

1: *Securing the thread*: Start by pulling needle through fabric back to front, leaving about 1" behind fabric. Hold this end with fingers as you begin stitching, and work over end with your first few stitches. After work is in progress, weave end through the back of a few stitches.

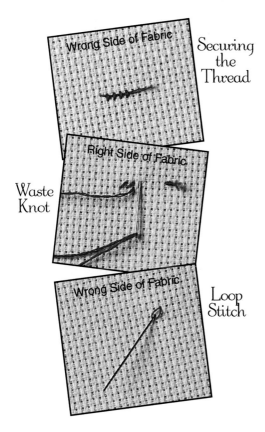

Securing the Thread

Waste Knot

Loop Stitch

2: *Waste knot*: Make a knot in end of floss and pull needle through fabric front to back several squares over from where your first cross-stitch will be. Come up at first stitch and stitch first few stitches over floss end. Clip knot.

3: *Loop stitch*: This method can only be used for even numbers of strands. Cut strands twice the normal length, then take half the number of strands needed and fold in half. Insert loose ends in needle and bring needle up from back at first stitch, leaving loop underneath. Take needle down through fabric and through loop; pull to secure.

For even stitches, keep a consistent tension on your thread, and pull thread and needle completely through fabric with each stab of the needle. Make all the top crosses on your cross-stitches face the same direction. To finish a thread, run the needle under the back side of several stitches and clip. Threads carried across the back of unworked areas may show through to the front, so do not carry threads.

Master Stitchery

Work will be neater if you always try to make each stitch by coming up in an unoccupied hole and going down in an occupied hole.

The sewing method is preferred for stitching on linen and some other evenweaves, but can also be used on Aida. Stitches are made as in hand sewing with needle going from front to back to front of fabric in one motion. All work is done from the front of the fabric. When stitching with the sewing method, it is important not to pull thread too tightly or stitches will become distorted. Stitching on linen is prettiest with the sewing method, using no hoop. If you use a hoop or frame when using the sewing method with Aida, keep in mind that fabric cannot be pulled taut. There must be "give" in the fabric in order for needle to slip in and out easily.

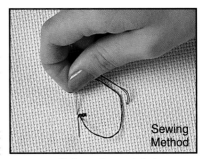

Sewing Method

In the stab method, needle and floss are taken completely through fabric twice with each stitch. For the first half of the stitch, bring needle up and pull thread completely through fabric to the front. Then take needle down and reach underneath and pull completely through to bottom.

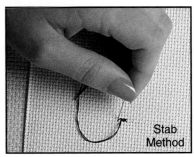

Stab Method

Working on Evenweave

When working on linen or other evenweave fabric, keep needle on right side of fabric, taking needle front to back to front with each stitch.

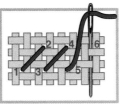

Work over two threads, placing the beginning and end of the bottom half of the first Cross-Stitch where a vertical thread crosses a horizontal thread.

Cleaning Your Needlework

Careful washing, pressing and sometimes blocking help preserve and protect your stitched piece. After stitching is complete, a gentle washing will remove surface dirt, hoop marks and hand oils that have accumulated on your fabric while stitching. Even if a piece looks clean, it's always a good idea to give it a nice cleaning before finishing. Never press your work before cleaning, as this only serves to set those hoop marks and soils that are best removed.

Using a gentle soap such as baby shampoo or gentle white dishwashing liquid and a large, clean bowl, make a solution of cool, sudsy water. If you use a handwash product, make sure the one you choose contains no chlorine bleach. Fill another bowl or sink with plain cool water for rinsing.

Soak your stitched piece in sudsy water for five to ten minutes. Then gently and without rubbing or twisting, squeeze suds through fabric several times. Dip piece several times in fresh cool water until no suds remain.

On rare occasions floss colors will run or fade slightly. When this happens, continue to rinse in cool water until water becomes perfectly clear. Remove fabric from water and lay on a soft, white towel. Never twist or wring your work. Blot excess water away and roll the piece up in the towel, pressing gently.

Never allow a freshly washed piece of embroidery to air dry. Instead, remove the damp piece from the towel and place face down on a fresh, dry white towel. To prevent color stains, it's important to keep the stitched piece flat, not allowing stitched areas to touch each other or other areas of the fabric. Make sure the edges of fabric are in straight lines and even. To be sure fabric edges are straight when pressing dry, use a ruler or T-square to check edges. Wash towel several times before using it to block cross-stitch, and use it only for this purpose.

After edges are aligned and fabric is perfectly smooth, cover the back of the stitched piece with a pressing cloth, cotton diaper or other lightweight white cotton cloth. Press dry with a dry iron set on a high permanent press or cotton setting, depending on fabric content. Allow stitchery to lie in this position several hours. Machine drying is acceptable after use for items like towels and kitchen accessories, but your work will be prettier and smoother if you give these items a careful pressing the first time.

Framing and Mounting

Shopping for Frames

When you shop for a frame, take the stitchery along with you and compare several frame and mat styles. Keep in mind the "feeling" of your stitched piece when choosing a frame. For example, an exquisite damask piece stitched with metallics and silk threads might need an ornate gold frame, while a primitive sampler stitched on dirty linen with flower thread would need a simpler, perhaps wooden frame.

Mounting

Cross-stitch pieces can be mounted on mat board, white cardboard, special padded or unpadded mounting boards designed specifically for needlework, or special acid-free mat board available from art supply stores. Acid-free framing materials are the best choice for projects you wish to keep well-preserved for future generations. If you prefer a padded look, cut quilt batting to fit mounting board.

Center blocked stitchery over mounting board of choice with quilt batting between, if desired. Leaving 1½" to 3" around all edges, trim excess fabric away along straight grain.

Mounting boards made for needlework have self-stick surfaces and require no pins. When using these products, lift and smooth needlework onto board until work is taut and edges are smooth and even. Turn board face down and smooth fabric to back, mitering corners.

Pins are required for other mounting boards. With design face up, keeping fabric straight and taut, insert a pin through fabric and edge of mounting board at the center of each side. Turn piece face down and smooth excess fabric to back, mitering corners.

There are several methods for securing fabric edges. Edges may be glued to mat board with liquid fabric glue or fabric glue stick. If mat board is thick, fabric may be stapled.

Mats & Glass

Pre-cut mats are available in many sizes and colors to fit standard-size frames. Custom mats are available in an even wider variety of colors, textures and materials. Using glass over cross-stitch is a matter of personal preference, but is generally discouraged. Moisture can collect behind glass and rest on fabric, causing mildew stains. A single or double mat will hold glass away from fabric.

Stitch Guide

Basic Stitchery

CROSS-STITCH (x):
There are two ways of making a basic Cross-Stitch. The first method is used when working rows of stitches in the same color. The first step makes the bottom half of the stitches across the row, and the second step makes the top half.

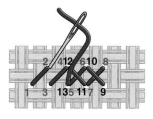

The second method is used when making single stitches. The bottom and top halves of each stitch are worked before starting the next stitch.

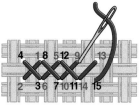

QUARTER CROSS-STITCH (¼x):
Stitch may slant in any direction.

THREE-QUARTER CROSS-STITCH (¾x): A Half Cross-Stitch plus a Quarter Cross-Stitch. May slant in any direction.

HALF CROSS-STITCH (½x): The first part of a Cross-Stitch. May slant in either direction.

Embellishing with Embroidery

EMBROIDERY stitches add detail and dimension to stitching. Unless otherwise noted, work Backstitches first, then other embroidery stitches.

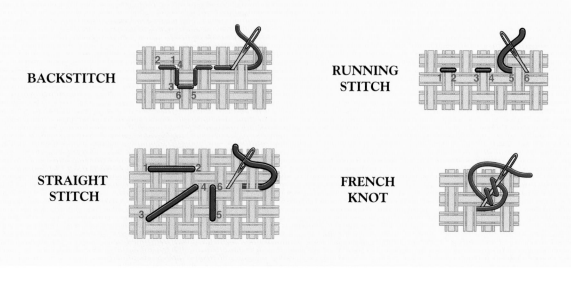

BACKSTITCH

RUNNING STITCH

STRAIGHT STITCH

FRENCH KNOT

Acknowledgments

We would like to express our appreciation to the many people who helped create this book. Our special thanks go to each of the talented designers who contributed original designs.

Our sincerest thanks and appreciation goes to the following manufacturers for generously providing their products for use in the following projects:

Charles Craft, Inc.
Aida: Apple of My Eye; Joe's Poem; Quilt Sampler; Sweet Peas
Linaida: Halloween
Fiddler's Cloth: I Collect Angels
Fiddler's Lite®: Where Love Abides

Creative Beginnings
Charms: Silver Belle

DMC®
Embroidery Floss: All Seasons Sampler; Angel Friends; Angel Rose; Apple of My Eye; Ark Sweet Ark; Autumn Angel; Birdhouse; Caution, Dust Bunny; Christmas Folk Art; Christmas Montage; Country Flowers; Country Ladies; Dino-Mite; Everything Is Beautiful; Fairies In Flowers; Fairy Reflections; Feathers & Flowers; Halloween; Harvest Welcome; Hummingbird & Heart; I Collect Angels; Joe's Poem; Joy to the World; Joy, Patience & Faith; Make a Joyful Noise; My Wife Said; Pumpkin Patch; Quilt Sampler; Shamrock Angel; Silver Belle; Sweet Peas; Trick or Treat; Turkey Whimsies; Warm Winter Memories; When I Prayed; Where Love Abides; Witty Kitties

Fairfield Processing Corp.
Soft Touch® Pillow Form: A Soft Answer; Christmas Folk Art; Fairies In Flowers

Fibre Craft
Jingle Bells: Silver Belle

Kreinik
Ribbon: Silver Belle
Very Fine (#4) Braid: Angel Friends

Mill Hill
Ceramic Buttons: Noah's Ark; Silver Belle
Seed Beads: Sweet Peas

Rainbow Gallery
Wisper Floss: Silver Belle

Offray
Ribbon: Autumn Angel

Sudberry House
Medium Tea Tray: Fairy Reflections

Warm & Natural®
Soft & Bright™ Needled Polyester Batting: Where Love Abides

Wichelt Imports, Inc.
Jobelan®: Everything Is Beautiful; Fairies In Flowers
Jobelan® Metallic: Silver Belle
Linen: Hummingbird & Heart

Continued

Acknowledgments

Continued

Zweigart®

Aida: All Seasons Sampler; Autumn Angel; Birdhouse; Country Ladies; Dino-Mite; Feathers & Flowers; Harvest Welcome; Joy, Patience & Faith; Pumpkin Patch; Turkey Whimsies

Damask Aida: Christmas Montage; Fairy Reflections

Dublin Linen: Country Flowers
Janina: Angel Friends
Jubilee: Angel Rose
Lugana®**:** Make a Joyful Noise; Shamrock Angel
Pastel Linen: Joy to the World
Vienna: Christmas Folk Art

Pattern Index

Designer Index